BEST OF

Prague

Richard Watkins

Best of Prague
2nd edition – March 2004

First published – May 2002

Published by Lonely Planet Publications Pty Ltd
ABN 36 005 607 983

Australia Head Office, Locked Bag 1, Footscray, Vic 3011
☎ 03 8379 8000 fax 03 8379 8111
🖥 talk2us@lonelyplanet.com.au
USA 150 Linden St, Oakland, CA 94607
☎ 510 893 8555 toll free 800 275 8555
fax 510 893 8572
🖥 info@lonelyplanet.com
UK 72–82 Rosebery Avenue, London EC1R 4RW
☎ 020 7841 9000 fax 020 7841 9001
🖥 go@lonelyplanet.co.uk
France 1 rue du Dahomey, 75011 Paris
☎ 01 55 25 33 00 fax 01 55 25 33 01
🖥 bip@lonelyplanet.fr
🖥 www.lonelyplanet.fr

This title was commissioned in Lonely Planet's London
office and produced by: **Commissioning Editor** Tim
Ryder & Judith Bamber **Coordinating Editor** Kalya Ryan
Coordinating Cartographer Valentina Kremenchutskaya
Layout Designer Sonya Brooke **Editors** Jocelyn Harewood
& Diana Saad **Managing Cartographer** Mark Griffiths
Cover Designer Annika Roojun **Project Manager** Eoin
Dunlevy **Series Designer** Gerilyn Attebery **Mapping
Development** Paul Piaia **Regional Publishing Manager**
Katrina Browning **Thanks to** Yvonne Bischofberger, Sally
Darmody, Bruce Evans, Ryan Evans, Mark Germanchis,
Cris Gibcus, Mark Griffiths, Ben Handicott, Martin Heng,
Yukiyoshi Kamimura, Chris Lee Ack, Adriana Mammarella,
Wayne Murphy, Charles Rawlings-Way, Lachlan Ross &
Gerard Walker.

ISBN 1 74059 478 9

Printed through Colorcraft Ltd, Hong Kong.

HOW TO USE THIS BOOK

Colour-Coding & Maps

Each chapter has a colour code along the
banner at the top of the page which is also
used for text and symbols on maps (eg, all
venues reviewed in the Highlights chapter
are orange on the maps). The fold-out
maps inside the front and back covers are
numbered from 1 to 8. All sights and venues
in the text have map references; eg, (5, B2)
means Map 5, grid reference B2. See p128 for
map symbols.

Prices

Multiple prices listed with reviews (eg $10/5)
usually indicate adult/concession admission to
a venue. Concession prices can include senior,
student, member or coupon discounts. Meal
cost and room rate categories are listed at
the start of the Eating and Sleeping chapters,
respectively.

Text Symbols

☎ telephone
✉ address
🖥 email/website address
$ admission
🕰 opening hours
ⓘ information
Ⓜ metro
🚊 tram
Ⓟ parking available
♿ wheelchair access
&#9ltimes; on site/nearby eatery
♿ child-friendly venue
Ⓥ good vegetarian selection

Contents

From the Publisher

AUTHOR

Richard Watkins

Richard was born and bred in Wales and after five years studying decided he'd like to see more of the world, which he's now been doing for several years. On his first trip to Prague, Richard was immediately captivated by the Czech capital's preponderance for off-the-wall surrealism, cool jazz, grand opera and cheap beer, and is already looking forward to sampling it all again.

Thanks are due to staff at the Czech Embassy in London and the Czech Tourist Authority. Also to Jaroslava Nováková at the Prague Information Centre, Jaromír Kubúo at Karlštejn Castle, and Jane Rawson.

The 1st edition of this book was written by Paul Smitz.

PHOTOGRAPHER

Richard Nebeský

Richard was not born with a camera in his hand; however, it wasn't long before his father, an avid photo enthusiast, gave him his first happy snap-unit. Ever since then the camera has been by his side. Richard has researched written and photographed for numerous Lonely Planet guides as well as for various magazines and other travel guide book publishers. He has also been commissioned to photograph Amsterdam and Prague twice for the respective Lonely Planet city guides.

SEND US YOUR FEEDBACK

We love to hear from travellers – your comments keep us on our toes and help make our books better. Our well-travelled team reads every word on what you loved or loathed about this book. Although we cannot reply individually to postal submissions, we always guarantee that your feedback goes straight to the appropriate authors, in time for the next edition – and the most useful submissions are rewarded with a free book. To send us your updates – and find out about LP events, newsletters and travel news – visit our award-winning website 🖳 www.lonelyplanet.com.

Note: We may edit, reproduce and incorporate your comments in Lonely Planet products such as guidebooks, websites and digital products, so let us know if you don't want your comments. For a copy of our privacy policy visit 🖳 www.lonelyplanet.com/privacy.

Introducing Prague

Prague, with its magnificent castle, Gothic towers, baroque churches, cobble-stoned lanes and Art Nouveau architecture, is one of Europe's most visually stunning cities. Long hidden from the outside world behind the Iron Curtain, since the fall of communism it has opened up to an ever-growing number of foreign visitors and is today a hugely popular tourist destination. With over 1000 years of history, this venerable

city, right at the heart of Europe, has seen more than its share of drama, from its medieval 'golden age', through its 16th-century glory days as capital of the Holy Roman Empire, to the Nazi and Soviet dictatorships of the 20th-century. It was only in 1993 that the modern Czech Republic was formed, with Prague as its capital, while in 2004, the country joins the European Union.

Prague is a prosperous, orderly and cosmopolitan city, whose laid-back citizens like nothing better than relaxing with a beer or two in one of the countless pubs. Innovative art galleries, museums, churches and synagogues jostle for your attention, while music is everywhere, from the Charles Bridge buskers to the many classical concerts, jazz clubs and international pop acts around town. In fact, there's so much going on you'll have trouble deciding just how much you can cram into one visit.

Reflections on Vltava River at Smetanova Embankment, with towers of Old Town Mill.

Neighbourhoods

Prague sits astride the Czech Republic's longest river, the Vltava, and is divided into ten districts, each comprising a number of suburbs. The compact historical centre (Praha 1) is the hub of most tourist activity and is itself made up of five distinct neighbourhoods. At the heart of Prague is **Staré Město** (Old Town), stretching from the Vltava east to náměstí Republiky, north to Široká and Dlouhá, and south to Národní, 28.října and Na Příkopě. Centred on Staroměstské náměstí (Old Town Square), is where you'll find the Astronomical Clock and the Týn Church, with its cobblestone lanes threading their way towards Charles Bridge. To the north is **Josefov**, centre of Prague's Jewish community. The main draw here is the Old-New Synagogue and the Jewish Museum. South and east of the Old Town lies **Nové Město** (New Town), a commercial area with more recent historical attractions such as the National Museum, plus lively clubs, bars and restaurants west of the city's main shopping drag, Wenceslas Square.

Vinohrady, southeast of the main train station, is fast becoming a hip place to hang out, with lots of fashionable eateries and bars, and a growing number of top-end shops. To the northeast is **Žižkov**, an edgy industrial suburb with new alternative-scene credentials. South of New Town is Prague's ethereal second castle, **Vyšehrad**, and across the river is a grunge-infested industrial enclave, **Smíchov**.

> ## Off the Beaten Track
> Though Prague often seems overwhelmed by seemingly endless numbers of foreign visitors, escaping the madding crowd is just a matter of a short metro and/or tram ride.
> Try the still, leafy grounds of **Vyšehrad** (p33) for a quick trip that can feel like a weekend away or better still, the vast grounds of **Stromovka** (p33) where camera-happy crowds are thankfully unknown. If you're in search of liquid refreshment away from the tour groups, drop by **U Osla v Kolébce** (p83). The **Lapidárium** (p25) is a stony treat, while a glimpse of **Church of the Most Sacred Heart of Our Lord** (p31) can become an investigation of sophisticated Vinohrady or the back-blocks of real-life Žižkov.

Enjoying the day in pretty Malá Strana

Directly north sits **Malá Strana** (Small Quarter), a warren of picturesque streets and stunning vistas, not to mention a lively restaurant scene.

Further northwest are the heights of **Hradčany**, dominated by the spectacular castle. Northeast of here, on the Vltava's 'big bend', is the parkland swathe of **Letná**, which is bordered in the northwest by a one-time fishing village that now features parks and residential areas, **Bubeneč**. Finally, in the northeast, you'll enjoy an eclectic mix of fairgrounds, galleries and cheap accommodation in **Holešovice**.

Itineraries

Prague is one of Europe's best preserved medieval cities, with an unrivalled wealth of baroque and Art Nouveau architecture; good enough reasons why Unesco added the city's historic centre to its World Cultural Heritage list in 1992. Prague has some truly outstanding sights, like the hilltop magnificence of Prague Castle, the spires of Týn Church poking above the rooftops, and the stately elegance of Charles Bridge.

Seeing it all – or even more than a fraction of it – isn't practical on a brief trip, but below are some ideas to get you acquainted with some of the best this exciting city has to offer. Students and children get discounts at most tourist attractions, and on public transport, while the Prague Card (690/560Kč) provides unlimited transport and admission to most of the main attractions for three days. It's available at the airport, Muzeum metro station, American Express (Václavské náměstí 56), and a number of information centres and hotels. Some museums and galleries have free days, while youth ID cards like ISIC and Euro26 will get you discounts at many places.

> **Prague Lowlights**
> - Blister-inducing cobblestones
> - Lack of air-conditioning in public buildings
> - Dodging shuffling crowds of camcorder-wielding tourists in the Old Town
> - Sauerkraut
> - Grumpy service
> - The proliferation of tacky souvenir shops
> - Stag parties

Awaiting the moment on Charles Bridge

One Day
Head straight to Old Town Square, and marvel at the Astronomical Clock. Cross Charles Bridge and climb to the imposing Prague Castle, where St Vitus Cathedral and the Garden on the Ramparts await. Make your way back to Malostranské náměstí and take in a concert at St Nicholas Church.

Two Days
Walk up Pařížská for a tour of Josefov, exploring the synagogues and the Old Jewish Cemetery. Take a leisurely walk back through Týn Court to the Municipal House for coffee or treat yourself to dinner at Francouzská.

Three Days
Wander down Wenceslas Square, maybe calling in at Dobré čajovny for a refreshing cup of tea. Cast an eye over the exhibits in the National Museum and in the evening book yourself a box at the State Opera or the National Theatre.

Highlights

PRAGUE CASTLE (5, B2)

Every city usually has several places clamouring to be rated the major drawcard, but in Prague there's no argument. With its magnificent cliff-top outlook, an 1100-year history going back to a simple walled-in compound in the 9th century, and a breathtaking scale that qualifies it as the biggest ancient castle in the world, **Prague Castle** (Pražský Hrad) is the indisputable centre-piece of the Czech capital.

INFORMATION

- ☎ 224 373 368, 224 372 434
- 🖳 www.hrad.cz
- ✉ Hradčany
- 💲 220/110Kč Ticket A (St Vitus Cathedral, Old Royal Palace, Basilica of St George, Powder Tower & Golden Lane); 180/90Kč Ticket B (St Vitus Cathedral, Old Royal Palace & Golden Lane); 40Kč Ticket C (Golden Lane); grounds free admission
- 🕑 historic buildings 9am-5pm Apr-Oct, 9am-4pm Nov-Mar; grounds 5am-midnight Apr-Oct, 6am-11pm Nov-Mar
- ℹ️ information centre open 9am-5pm Apr-Oct, 9am-4pm Nov-Mar; audio guide 200/250Kč 2/3hrs; guided tours 80Kč 9am-4pm Tue-Sun
- Ⓜ Malostranská; Hradčanská
- ♿ limited
- ✕ Café Poet (p63)

The castle has undergone regular renovations since the first fortifications went up, starting in the 12th century with the Romanesque features added by Prince Sobešlav I, through to the mid-16th century planting of the **Royal Garden** (p33) and construction of the Renaissance **Summer Palace** (p28) then up to and beyond the consecration of **St Vitus Cathedral** (p10) in 1929. It remains the Czech seat of power and official residence of the president, though current incumbent Václav Klaus has chosen to live elsewhere, as a matter of practicality.

Star sights include the main gate on **Hradčanské náměstí** (p34) where a regimented changing of the guards happens on the hour, the **Old Royal Palace** (p26), site of the infamous 'defenestration', the Czech history exhibition in **Lobkowicz Palace** (p25), the **Basilica of St George** (p31), and the collection of Bohemian art in the **Convent of St George** (p27). Other points of interest include the **Toy Museum** (p38), the **Powder Tower** (p26), and the **Garden on the Ramparts** (p32).

DON'T MISS

- cottages of Golden Lane
- excellent exhibitions at Prague Castle Gallery
- watching the changing of the guard, to music reminiscent of a '60s TV puppet show
- the view from the 'defenestration' window in the Old Royal Palace

CHARLES BRIDGE (4, B3)

When a flood completely destroyed Judith Bridge in 1357, work began immediately on another bridge across the Vltava. The project was completed in 1402, and for the next 460-odd years **Charles Bridge** (Karlův most) was the only structure spanning the river. The 520m sandstone edifice was originally called (creatively) Stone Bridge, until it was bequeathed the name of its original commissioner, Charles IV, in 1870. The severe 2002 flood caused immense damage to property on both sides of the river, while Charles Bridge itself stood up to the waters and emerged relatively unscathed.

INFORMATION

✉ Karlův most, Staré Město

ⓘ Prague Information Service office at the bridge tower on the Malá Strana side of the Vltava

Ⓜ Staroměstská

♿ good

✖ Kampa Park (p66)

A common story told about the bridge's construction is that egg yolk was mixed into its mortar to make it sturdier – the weight-resistant qualities of egg yolk having obviously been well documented – and that eggs were sent to Prague by helpful citizens from all over the region (apparently one particularly helpful town had them hard-boiled so they wouldn't break on the way).

Of the many interesting figures lining the bridge's sides, the first erected was the bronze statue of St John of Nepomuk, Czech patron saint, who found himself on the wrong side during a messy court intrigue and ended up lifeless in the Vlatava at the behest of bad King Wenceslas IV in 1393. Other monuments include several of St Wenceslas, St Jude (patron saint of lost causes) and a Crucifix with a gilded Hebrew inscription, which was funded by the fine of a 17th-century Jew who had allegedly mocked it. The bridge was renovated in the 1970s and turned into a pedestrian zone. At either end is a tower, both open to visitors and commanding incredible views from their roofs.

Charles Bridge represents the best and worst of Prague. At its 'worst', it's sardine-packed with people shuffling and elbowing and congregating around souvenir stalls and buskers; you can be so distracted getting across that you forget to actually look at the bridge

DON'T MISS
• night-time view of a glowing Prague, with silhouetted statues in the foreground
• listening to a jazz band in the early evening
• the view from the Staré Město bridge tower

or its magnificent view. The 'best' is a combination of the bridge's captivating physical form and the community feel that can often emanate from the collective of locals, foreigners and musicians who inhabit it. Look out for the hepcats of the Charles Bridge Swing Band and the elderly gent in black and his mean sax.

ST VITUS CATHEDRAL

(8, C2)

St Vitus Cathedral (Katedrála Sv Víta) towers above the third courtyard of Prague Castle, primed to use its enormous Gothic stature to intimidate visitors wandering in from the main gate. Equipped with a lofty 100m main tower, and adorned with an amazing 10.5m diameter rose window, this is the largest cathedral in the Czech Republic, a fact that helps explain why it took centuries to get this awesome beast from the drawing board to reality. Emperor Charles IV initiated its construction in 1344 on the site of a 10th-century rotunda, but it wasn't until thousands of pieces of glass had been painstakingly set in the large west-facing rose window in 1929 that St Vitus was finally finished.

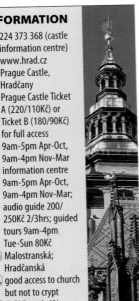

INFORMATION

- ☎ 224 373 368 (castle information centre)
- 🖳 www.hrad.cz
- ✉ Prague Castle, Hradčany
- 💲 Prague Castle Ticket A (220/110Kč) or Ticket B (180/90Kč) for full access
- 🕑 9am-5pm Apr-Oct, 9am-4pm Nov-Mar
- ℹ information centre 9am-5pm Apr-Oct, 9am-4pm Nov-Mar; audio guide 200/250Kč 2/3hrs; guided tours 9am-4pm Tue-Sun 80Kč
- Ⓜ Malostranská; Hradčanská
- ♿ good access to church but not to crypt
- ✗ Café Poet (p63)

The cathedral's huge nave is encircled by side-chapels, the most striking of which is the **Chapel of St Wenceslas** complete with precious, glittering stonework. Not to be outdone, however, is the ultra-baroque silver tomb of **St John of Nepomuk**, surrounded by silver angels. Beneath the floor of the cathedral is the **Royal Crypt**, a tight space (particularly when jammed with fellow visitors) with a view to the stately 1930s sarcophagi of Charles IV, Wenceslas IV, Rudolf II and George of Poděbrady. If you have a head for heights, you might care to scale the tower for the great views at the top, but be prepared for 287 slow, strenuous steps.

Stained in Style

St Vitus Cathedral is blessed with some exemplary stained-glass windows. Most spectacular is that by Art Nouveau artist **Alfons Mucha** (1909) in the New Archbishop's Chapel. For some of the oldest examples, see the three windows in the Chapel of St Antony (1865-6); for one of the newest, see the window in the southern wall of the Chapel of St Wenceslas (1968).

OLD TOWN SQUARE (7, C2)

The geographical hub of the Old Town, **Staroměstské Náměstí**, is also one of the tourist hubs of Prague. On any given day, regardless of the weather or time (except early morning), you'll find people streaming across the paving from every direction to take seats at the overpriced outdoor restaurants and bars, mass patiently in front of the **Astronomical Clock** (p14), or sit on benches around the **statue of Jan Hus** (p29) to take in the view or assess the latest footage on hand-held videos.

INFORMATION

✉ Staroměstské náměstí, Staré Město
Ⓜ Staroměstská; Můstek
♿ good
✖ U Rotta (p75)

Sometimes called Staromák, the square became Prague's central marketplace in the late 12th century, taking the commercial baton from a marketplace that was sited where the thoroughfare of Široká is today. This job description lasted for over seven centuries, in which time a plethora of architectural styles found homes around the square's perimeter. Some of the most prominent examples include the Gothic **Church of Our Lady Before Týn** (p16); the late baroque-constructed but rococo-swathed **Kinský Palace** (p27); the

Autumn Festival in the Old Town Square

House of the Stone Bell, with its Gothic facade underneath a pastel baroque facing; and, on the southern side of the square, the gay neo-Renaissance frontage of **Štorch House**.

A Date with History

1338 John of Luxembourg establishes town hall
1422 Hussite preacher Jan Želivský executed
1458 Hussite George of Poděbrady elected King of Bohemia in Town Hall
1915 6 July – Statue commemorating the 500th anniversary of the martyrdom of Jan Hus unveiled
1945 8 May – Withdrawing German troops try to destroy town hall
1948 21 February – Klement Gottwald proclaims communist government from Kinský balcony
1968 21 August – Warsaw Pact tanks end 'Prague Spring'

CENTRE FOR MODERN & CONTEMPORARY ART (6, C2)

The huge **Trade Fair Palace** (Veletržní palác) in Holešovice hosts one of Prague's most extensive art collections. The rather bland glass and concrete 'palace' was built in 1928, in the new 'functionalist' style which, as its name suggests, rejected ornamentation in favour of unadorned practicality. The stark and spacious white interior, though, provides an ideal setting for displays of artworks from the 19th century to the present day.

INFORMATION

- ☎ 224 301 111
- 🖳 smsu@ngprague.cz, www.ngprague.cz
- ✉ Dukelských hrdinů 47, Holešovice
- 💲 250/120Kč for all 4 levels, 200/100Kč choice of 3 levels, 150/70Kč for 2 levels, 100/50Kč for 1 level, free 1st Wed of month
- 🕙 10am-6pm Tue-Sun (to 9pm Thu)
- ℹ Internet cafe off the foyer
- Ⓜ Vltavská
- ♿ good
- 🍴 Corso (p77)

There are four permanent collections on show, displayed on floors 1 to 4 (the ground floor and the Mezzanine floor above host temporary exhibitions, as, occasionally, does level 5). Level 1 is devoted to **20th-century foreign art**, including works by Picasso, Edvard Munch, Joan Miró and Oskar Kokoschka; look out for his surreal satire on the lead-up to WWII, *The Red Egg*. Level 2 provides a fascinating overview of **20th-century Czech art**, from the engaging fantasies of František Janoušek, to the Marvel Comics-style 'socialist realism' of Eduard Stavinoha and the bizarre symbolism of what came to be known as 'Czech Grotesque', a satirical art movement that grew up under the communist regime. Check out the Czech abstract and cubist works – including some striking furniture – in the **1900-1930 art** display on level 3. Keep an eye out too for Jan Zrzavý's *Cleopatra*, imagined as a kind of shiny red jelly-baby reclining on a couch. Also on this floor is the excellent collection of **19th- and early 20th-century French art**, with bronzes by Rodin and paintings by Gauguin, Monet, Renoir and other leading lights. Level 4 showcases **19th-century Czech art**, with many idyllic and idealised landscapes. Bedřich Havránek's finely detailed *By the Brook*

DON'T MISS
- Gustav Klimt's *Virgins*
- František Kupka's symbolist works, *Path of Silence* and *Babylon*
- cubist furniture by Josef Gočár
- Loir Luigi's evocative *Underground Railway*
- Rodin's male nude, *The Bronze Age*

and Antonín Gareis's *Village Fair* are typical of this rural nostalgia.

The one downside to this gallery is that there's so much to see, and you could easily spend the whole day here. Fortunately your ticket allows you to leave the building and return later on, if you fancy stepping out for lunch. Take your time and relish all that the museum has to offer.

MUNICIPAL HOUSE (7, F2)

Few buildings in Prague can elicit the delight that many visitors feel when they first lay their eyes on the exuberant facade of the **Municipal House** (Obecní Dům). The 500-room landmark was built between 1905 and 1912 on the site of King's Court, the official Bohemian monarch's residence from the late 14th century until the Hapsburgs moved into the area in 1526. It was intended to be suitably impressive as the architectural representative of Prague, and so a collective of leading painters and sculptors were commissioned to create an Art Nouveau masterpiece; among the famous names who contributed were Alfons Mucha, Karel Špillar, Josef Myslbek and Jan Preisler.

INFORMATION

☎ 222 002 100
🖳 www.obecni-dum.cz
✉ náměstí Republiky 5, Staré Město
💲 guided tours 150Kč
🕗 7.30am–11pm
ℹ guided tours from information centre (open 10am–6pm); classical concerts in Smetana Hall
Ⓜ Náměstí Republiky
♿ good
✗ Kavárna obecní dům (p73); Francouzská (p73)

While the facade is amazing enough, festooned as it is with sculpted allegorical figures, taking centre stage inside (literally) is the biggest concert hall in town, **Smetana Hall**. Dripping with frescoes, sculptures and natural light from the original skylights, it was here that Czechoslovak independence was declared in 1918. Just off the

DON'T MISS
• Jan Preisler's murals in the Oriental Salon
• ceramic tiling lining the stairwell to the basement
• coffee in Kavárna obecní dům
• the Prague Symphony Orchestra in Smetana Hall (p90)

Mosiac above entrance, to welcome you

hall are the restored **Ladies' Withdrawing Room** and Moroccan-style **Oriental Salon**. The **Mayor's Salon** is a veritable gallery of Mucha's work, dominated by the ceiling fresco *Slavic Concorde*, which depicts an eagle metaphorically held aloft by Czech-personified human virtues. He also designed the stained-glass windows and curtains. Further along is the **Rieger Hall**, where Havel and others worked out the handover of power with the communists in 1989.

The Art Nouveau theme is continued in the Hall's three restaurants, most notably in the upmarket **Francouzská**, with a lighter touch in the more casual *kavárna* (cafe).

OLD TOWN HALL & ASTRONOMICAL CLOCK (7, C2)

The 1338 **Town Hall** of Staré Město (Staroměstská Radnice) is a complex of local homes that were incorporated and rebuilt over many years. One of the most famous is at the Malé náměstí end: the sgraffito-covered building that once housed a young Franz Kafka. Perched on the tower is the beautifully styled **Astronomical Clock**, a 1490 device by a certain Master Hanuš, with an upper face graced with representations of astronomical movement and external figurines joined on the hour by a parade of apostles for a brief and extremely popular mechanical show.

Inside, most visitors charge straight for the 60m tower, which offers an excellent perspective on the mosaic of people in the square below. On the 1st floor is the **Gothic chapel** and the **Hall of the Mayors of the City**. The chapel was consecrated in 1381 in the names of Czech patron saints Wenceslas, Vitus and Ludmila, and has a lovely oriel colourfully streaked by

DON'T MISS

- view of clock's apostles from Gothic chapel
- watching the wooden apostles nod past on the hour
- gawping at the size of the crowd gawping at the clock

Astronomical Clock where you lose time

stained glass. The Hall of Mayors is a dry affair, with a collection of portraits of mainly 18th-century civic chiefs. Accessible from the ground floor are the **Romanesque and Gothic historic halls**, housing temporary art and photographic exhibitions.

Huge crowds gather well in advance to watch the clock put on its little show on the hour, though it's something of an anticlimax watching the wooden dummies quickly glide past the two opened windows. Nevertheless, it rarely fails to elicit 'oohs', 'aahs' and camera flashes from the expectant spectators.

NATIONAL MUSEUM (4, G6)

The brooding bulk of the **National Museum** (Národní Muzeum), with its vast natural history and archaeology collections, rears up at the southern end of Wenceslas Square. Established as the Patriotic Museum in 1818, the museum is the oldest in the Czech Republic, and has occupied this enviable site since 1891.

Viewed from the upper levels, the cavernous atrium, radiating several grand staircases, bears an unnerving resemblance to some of the spatial illusions and impossible structure etchings created by Dutch artist MC Escher, such as Relativity and Concave and Convex. Up these spatially intact stairs the galleries begin with the **Pantheon**, filled with the bronze likenesses of prominent Czechs such as Jan Hus and Dvořák. The fusty and seemingly endless **mineralogy** section can cause drowsiness, with row after row of cabinets with Czech-only labels. Calcite fans will have plenty to feast their eyes on though. More engaging is the **zoology** section with its stuffed, glassy-eyed residents, fossils and gigantic fin whale skeleton, and the **archaeology** galleries, with artefacts spanning the Neolithic to the Middle Ages, including some intricate bronze jewellery and fine pottery.

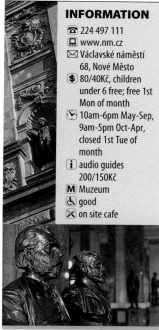

INFORMATION

☎ 224 497 111
🖥 www.nm.cz
✉ Václavské náměstí 68, Nové Město
💲 80/40Kč, children under 6 free; free 1st Mon of month
🕐 10am-6pm May-Sep, 9am-5pm Oct-Apr, closed 1st Tue of month
ℹ audio guides 200/150Kč
Ⓜ Muzeum
♿ good
✕ on site cafe

Statues keep watch in National Museum

The tiny **anthropology** section has a gruesome collection of human skulls showing various diseases. Temporary exhibitions have followed such curiously diverse themes as Japanese theatrical costumes and the history of Czech radio, while the atrium is also a venue for regular concerts.

Student Power

It was in front of the National Museum on 16 January 1969 that the 21-year-old Charles University student **Jan Palach** made the ultimate sacrifice in protest against the Soviet invasion and occupation of his country. Setting himself on fire, he stumbled down the steps in flames and collapsed at the bottom; a cross in the pavement marks the spot where he fell. He died in hospital four days later, and has since been honoured with the renamed **Jan Palach Square** (p34).

CHURCH OF OUR LADY BEFORE TÝN (7, D2)

Rising up behind the Týnská School (actually a parish school until the mid-19th century) is the hallowed mass of the **Church of Our Lady Before Týn** (Kostel Panny Marie Před Týnem), its exterior bristling with dramatic Gothic touches. The cathedral is an Old Town Square landmark with distinctive twin spires that are a reassuring sight to many tourists after losing their bearings (again) in the narrow surrounding byways.

INFORMATION

- ✉ Staroměstské náměstí, Staré Město
- $ free
- ☾ services 4.30pm Mon-Fri, 1pm Sat, 11.30am & 9pm Sun
- ⓘ occasional concerts
- Ⓜ Staroměstská; Můstek
- ♿ good (entry from Celetná)
- ✂ Ebel Coffee House (p73)

Construction on Týn church began in 1380 to replace another chapel, but the building contract apparently didn't specify an end date, as subsequent years saw the completion of items such as the roof (1457), gable (1463), southern tower (1511), and a new northern tower (1835).

DON'T MISS

- tomb of Tycho Brahe
- rococo altar at northern end
- Karel Škretäs' altar artwork
- the sound of the renovated 17th-century pipe organ during concerts

The Church from the Old Town Square

The church was initially one of the strongholds of **Hussitism**, the church-reform movement championed by Jan Hus in the late 14th and early 15th centuries, but eventually succumbed to Catholicism and the lavish worship of baroque interior design.

Anyone unaccustomed to the sheer immodesty of baroque decor should be warned that the first glimpse of the Church of Our Lady Before Týn's massive interior, replete with imposing statuary and incredibly ornate altars, will probably come as something of a saccharine shock.

People sometimes circumnavigate the church puzzling over where to find the correct entry – you'll be able to access it at the far end of the passageway that opens up beside Café Italia on the Old Town Square, although the church is only open for services, not tourist visits.

STRAHOV MONASTERY (2, B3)

The giant white **Strahov Monastery** (Strahovský Klášter) looks down from its Petřín Hill vantage point over the densest part of Malá Strana, a serene view which gives its grounds an extra-meditative quality. The monastery was established in 1140 by Prince Vladislav II for the Premonstratensians, followers of the teachings of St Augustine, but the complex didn't undergo its most significant developments (including the reconstruction of a brewery) until the 17th and 18th centuries.

The highlight of a visit to Strahov, apart from the inherent pleasure in just getting to its delightful location, is its **library**, comprising one of the oldest monastic collections in the country. Researchers get access to many of the age-bleached books and manuscripts. Others have to be content with glimpses of the 50,000 tomes in the baroque, double-storey **Philosophy Hall**, built in 1794 and decorated with a fresco by Anton Maulbertsch, and the 16,000 books of the

INFORMATION

☎ library 220 516 671, museum 224 511 137
✉ Strahovské nádvoří 1, Strahov
$ library 60/40Kč, gallery 35/20Kč, museum 30/15Kč
🕐 library 9am–noon & 1–5pm, museum 9am–5pm Tue–Sun, gallery 9am–noon & 12.30–5pm Tue–Sun
ℹ library viewed by tour only
Ⓜ Malostranská, then tram 22 or 23 to Pohořelec
✕ Oživlé Dřevo (p63)

DON'T MISS
• 9th-century jewel-encrusted Strahov gospel (library)
• the staff of Jeroným II, former Strahov abbot (gallery)
• being confused by the preserved fruit and weird sea creatures in the 'Dept of Curiosities'

equally stunning **Theology Hall**. The **gallery** (p28) has a fascinating collection of monastic paintings and sculptures from Bohemia and elsewhere in Europe, including early-19th-century Czech masters and Dutch, Flemish and Italian 17th- to 18th-century painters.

If you've yet to have your fill of weighty baroque, have a look at the interior of the **Church of the Assumption of Our Lady**, built in 1143. There's also a **Museum of Czech Literature** here, though the inherently interesting assorted manuscripts and temporary exhibitions don't make a lot of sense unless you can read Czech.

Philosophy Hall in Monastery Library

LORETA (2, B2)

The **Loreta** is a significant and splendid pilgrimage site established by Baroness Benigna Katharina von Lobkowicz in 1626 and subsequently maintained and protected by the Capuchins, an order associated with St Francis of Assisi's brotherhood. Its spiritual centrepiece is a replica of **Santa Casa**, the house of the Virgin Mary in Palestine that stood in Nazareth before being dismantled by pilgrims and shipped to Loreto in Italy in 1294. Legend has it that angels provided the transportation, but this could have something to do with the name of the family who patronised the house-moving – Angeli.

The Santa Casa copy, complete with original fresco fragments and the wonder-working statue (its actual name) of **Our Lady of Loreto**, sits in a fine courtyard surrounded by chapel-lined arcades. The Church of the Nativity of Our Lord has a deliriously baroque

INFORMATION

- ☎ 220 516 740
- ✉ Loretánské náměstí 7, Hradčany
- $ 80/60Kč
- ☽ 9am-12.15pm & 1-4.30pm Tue-Sun
- ℹ services 7.30am Sat, 6pm Sun
- Ⓜ Malostranská, then tram 22 or 23 to Pohořelec
- ✖ Malý Buddha (p63)

DON'T MISS

- 'Prague Sun' monstrance and its 6000-plus diamonds in the Treasury
- 27-bell carillon at entrance playing on the hour
- *Presentation in the Temple* fresco in the Church of the Nativity of Our Lord

altar, a rococo organ and some beautiful frescoes; the side altars of Sts Felicissimus and Marcia contain the aristocratically dressed remains of two Spanish martyrs. In the south-western corner is the **Chapel of Our Lady of Sorrows**, which has a sculpture of a crucified bearded woman – apparently St Starosta successfully prayed for a beard to maintain her chastity, but her father had her crucified for thus derailing her arranged marriage.

Tours end with a glimpse inside **Loreto Treasury** and its breathtaking display of pilgrim- and patron-donated riches, including a wonderful altar made of ebony. If you need a breath of air after gazing at this lot, wander over to the scenic terraces beside Strahov Monastery.

VYŠEHRAD (6, C4)

According to legend, the first fortress was raised here in the 7th century by the Slavonic chieftain Krok, whose daughter, Libuše, went on to found Prague itself. Whatever the truth of the tale, **Vyšehrad** today is a pleasant excursion from the bustle of modern Prague, with extensive **gardens** (p33) to stroll through and splendid views over the Vlatava. And all just a swift metro ride from the city centre, followed by a short walk.

In the late 11th century, King Vratislav II chose Vyšehrad as the site for a palace, the **Church of Sts Peter & Paul**, and what is now the city's oldest Romanesque structure, **St Martin Rotunda**. But the subsequent rise of Prague Castle as the royal seat meant the decline of this southern stronghold. Charles IV resurrected Vyšehrad with a Gothic palace, but it was badly damaged during the Hussite wars. After a stint as an army garrison, the now-baroque fortress attracted lots of attention from 19th-century Romantic artists and nationalists; Smetana set his opera *Libuše* here. Since the 1920s, it has been a quiet park, popular with Prague families on the weekends.

The exuberant interior of the Church of Sts Peter and Paul is a surprisingly harmonious mixture of neo-Gothic, baroque and Art Nouveau, with typically stylish frescoes of saints and swirling botanical motifs by František and Marie Urban. Of special significance to Czechs is **Vyšehrad Cemetery**, containing the graves of well-known country folk like Dvořák, Smetana, Mucha and Čapek.

INFORMATION

✉ Soběslavova 2, Vyšehrad
$ grounds free; Church of Sts Peter & Paul 20/10Kč
☾ grounds open 24hr
ⓘ information centre just beyond Tábor Gate, approached from the metro station
Ⓜ Vyšehrad
♿ good
✗ U Vyšehradské Rotundy (p77)

Door detail at Church of Sts Peter & Paul

Stuff of Legends

Czech legends attempt to explain the birth of Prague in mythological terms, most (it's been theorised) constructed in the minds of social chroniclers. Vyšehrad features heavily in these stories, and this legendary status has made the old fortress a magnet for poets, painters and composers, particularly those who were working during the 19th-century resurgence of Czech culture (Czech National Revival) and sought an enigmatic icon to represent the Czech past.

MUSEUM OF DECORATIVE ARTS (4, C2)

Arts and Crafts fans may want to head for the neo-Renaissance building across the road from the Rudolfinum, where there's a fabulous historical catalogue of 16th- to early-20th-century domestic decorations.

Elaborate Museum facade

The **Museum of Decorative Arts** (Umělecko-Průmyslové Muzeum) was set up here in 1900 in an effort to spur on local ambition for the region's oft-criticised applied arts scene, which had become dominated by Industrial Revolution blandness. The museum has now amassed over 250,000 exemplary pieces, though you'll find only a fraction of these on display here.

Above reception is a hall for temporary exhibitions which are often well worth a look; they usually showcase works by young contemporary designers. But the main reason for visiting is the permanent top-floor exhibit called **The Story of Materials**. Here you'll find wonderful displays of glass, ceramics, tapestries and timepieces. There's also an exhibition

of ladies' fashions, from the prim and plain early 1800s to the garish 1960s and '70s, while on the level above is a collection of ecclesiastical garments dating back as far as the 14th century.

A small number of early books and prints and baroque and cubist furniture complete the small but fascinating displays. Part of the museum's magnificent horde of jewels is now on show at the prosaically named **Prague Jewellery Collection** (p26).

DON'T MISS
- the collection of Art Nouveau advertising posters
- 16th-century majolica
- stunning desks by Josef Danhauser and Josef Gočar
- stairwell ceiling and stained-glass windows

Modern poster advertises the Museum

OLD-NEW SYNAGOGUE (4, D2)

The **Old-New Synagogue** (Staronová Synagóga) is the oldest synagogue in Europe, erected in Gothic style around 1270 to serve as Prague's prime site of Jewish worship. Jews are thought to have settled in the city as early as the mid-10th century, though an area known as Jewish Town (later Josefov; p31) was not established until around 200 years later. Originally called the New or Great Shul, and subsequently labelled 'Old-New' once other synagogues appeared, the building on Červená is believed to have been predated by an important synagogue called Old Shul, which was torn down in 1867. The site of Old Shul is now occupied by the Moorish splendour of the **Spanish Synagogue** (p32).

INFORMATION

✉ Červená, Josefov
💲 200/140Kč
🕙 9.30am-6pm Sun-Thu, 9.30am-5pm Fri Apr-Oct; 9.30am-5pm Sun-Thu, 9.30am-2pm Fri Nov-Mar; closed on Jewish holidays
Ⓜ Staroměstská
✕ King Solomon (p64)

The Old-New Synagogue, which underwent restoration in 1998-9, has the twin naves typical of secular and sacred medieval architecture, and a half-dozen bays with ribbed vaulting. On the eastern wall is the **holy ark** in which the Torah scrolls are kept. In the centre of the synagogue is the **bimah** (raised platform supporting a pulpit), enclosed by a 15th-century iron grille, and on the walls are Hebrew biblical abbreviations.

Remember that if you want to enter the synagogue, men must have their heads covered – yarmulkes are handed out at the entrance, though hats or bandannas are allowable substitutes.

The Legend of Golem

Of the many rabbis that have preached here, **Rabbi Loew** is the most famous. Legend has it that Loew fashioned a living creature from clay, **Golem**, to help protect the Jewish community. However, Golem was unstable and after the rabbi forgot to give him his daily orders, he ran amok. Loew was forced to 'undo' him, after which he placed the now lifeless clay inside the synagogue, where the remains reputedly still lie.

NATIONAL THEATRE (4, C5)

One of Prague's more eye-catching buildings is the **National Theatre** (Národní Divadlo), particularly on a bright day when reflected sunlight blazes from the metal-sheathed roof – but it's more to Czech people than a landmark. The building emerged out of a cultural and political

INFORMATION

- ☎ 114 901 448
- 🖳 www.narodni -divadlo.cz
- ✉ Národní 2, Nové Město
- ⓘ box offices 10am- 6pm
- Ⓜ Národní Třída
- ♿ good
- 🍴 Café Slavia (p68)

Theatre goers wait for a performance

climate in the late 19th century that demanded mainstream presentation of Czech theatre, not just because no other large venue existed, but because the idea embodied the nationalistic spirit of the time. Backed by notables such as historian František Palacký and composer Bedřich Smetana, and designed by Josef Zítek, the theatre came to life in 1881 – only to promptly burn down. It reopened two years later.

Familiar Sounds

When the National Theatre reopened on 18 November 1883 after suffering a devastating fire, it did so to the strains of Bedrich Smetana's opera *Libuše*. In a nice bit of cultural synergy, the theatre reopened again exactly one century later (this time after six years of intensive restoration) to the same opera.

The building's internal and external decorations were the work of a number of well-known Czech artists, who achieved such prestige from their work that thereafter they were known as the 'National Theatre Generation'.

Note that there are two box offices, one in the main building, the other in the modern glass construction at the rear.

PETŘÍN HILL (5, A5)

Glorious though Prague's historic streets may be, sometimes you just want to get away from it all and swap the cobblestones for some soft turf. **Petřín Hill** (Petřinské Sady) is the large mound providing a natural backdrop to Malá Strana, and is an excellent place to play with the kids, read a book, or just wander the leafy trails that crisscross its surface.

If you've chosen to ride the **funicular** up from Újezd, you can either disembark halfway up the 318m hill or head to the terminus, where the 299 steps of **Petřín Tower** await. This 62m tower is a scale model (5:1) of the Eiffel Tower, built in 1891 for the Prague Exposition, and has spectacular views to accompany your huffs and puffs. Nearby, the kids (and some parents) will love distorting themselves in the **Maze** (p37), or checking out the **Štefánik Observatory**.

INFORMATION

- ✉ Petřín Hill, Malá Strana
- ⓘ funicular runs every 10min from 9am-11.30pm, costs 12/6Kč
- Ⓜ Národní Třída, then tram 22, 23 or 57 to Újezd
- ✕ Cantina (p66)

Hunger Wall – reminder of a bleak past

DON'T MISS
- walking along the Hunger Wall
- Church of St Lawrence's ceiling fresco
- stopping to take in city views
- letting yourself get lost

You just think you're lost in the Maze

Sometimes even the crowds up here can get to you, and weekends are best avoided if you have an aversion to queues. If you feel the onset of social exhaustion, follow the old fortifications southeast and head through the wall to the southern side of the hill. Here in peaceful **Kinský Gardens** you'll find lots of places to relax, and not too far in is the unique construction of the **Church of St Michael** (p31).

ST NICHOLAS CHURCH (5, C3)

There are three churches called St Nicholas in Prague, but only one that took 82 years and three generations of one family to build, and is regarded as an outstanding example of baroque architecture. This is the **St Nicholas Church** (Kostel Sv Mikuláše) located west of the Vltava that has greedily consumed most of the available space in Malostranské náměstí, and as an encore dominates the local skyline with its 70m-high verdigris dome.

INFORMATION

- ✉ Malostranské náměstí 38, Malá Strana
- 💲 50/25Kč, belfry 40/30Kč
- 🕐 8.30am-4.45pm; belfry 10am-6pm
- ℹ concerts usually at 6pm
- Ⓜ Malostranská
- ✖ U tří zlatých hvězd (p67)

Delightful frescoes and ornate columns

Work on the church was started by a Jesuit order in 1673, but it was a Dientzenhofer father-son act, plus a next generation son-in-law, who were directly responsible for the construction of the church, finally finished in 1755.

The incredible late-baroque interior is awash with gilt and marble, and contains numerous pillars,

Art Imitates Roof

The enormous ceiling fresco, *Apotheosis of St Nicholas* by Johann Lucas Kracker, is the largest in Europe. To check out its other claim to fame, head up to the gallery and look at how the painting has been skilfully rendered to blend near-perfectly with the ceiling architecture, so the two are practically inseparable.

frescoes and dramatically gesturing over-life-size statues of saints. One of the artists who had a hand in the 10 years' worth of interior decorating was Karel Škréta, who produced a painting for the chapel's main altar. Mozart ran his fingers over the 2500-pipe organ in 1787, and was honoured with a Requiem mass here after his death. If you're not feeling too giddy from the ornamentation, you can also climb the bell tower for an extra fee.

Sights & Activities

MUSEUMS

Army Museum (6, D3) The grim barrack-like building which houses this museum has seen better days, but the extensive collection of WWI and WWII uniforms, weapons and other Czech and foreign militaria are worth a look. More interesting, though, are the temporary exhibitions covering such subjects as the Heydrich assassination (see the boxed text 'Operation Anthropoid' p29).
☎ 973 204 924 ✉ U Památníku 2, Žižkov
💲 free 🕐 9.30am-6pm Tue-Sun Ⓜ Florenc
♿ limited

Ceremonial Hall (4, C2) Formerly the Old Jewish Cemetery mortuary (p30) and now part of the Jewish Museum, the Ceremonial Hall (Obřadní Síň) is the site of an interesting exhibition on Jewish traditions relating mainly to illness and death; the rest of the exhibit is next door in Klaus Synagogue.
☎ 222 317 191 🖥 www.jewishmuseum.cz
✉ U starého hřbitova 3a, Josefov 💲 Jewish Museum 300/200Kč
🕐 9am-4.30pm Sun-Fri Nov-Mar; 9am-6pm Sun-Fri Apr-Oct; closed Jewish holidays Ⓜ Staroměstská

Czech Museum of Fine Arts (7, B3) This easily overlooked little gallery on the corner of Karlova and Husova is actually an exhibition space for rotating displays of innovative contemporary artworks, following various themes. It's worth the entry fee just to see the old ladies who look after the place jump to life and show you how to work the interactive installations.
☎ 222 220 418 ✉ Husova 19–21, Staré Město 💲 50/20Kč
🕐 10am-6pm Tue-Sun Ⓜ Staromestská

Jewish Museum (4, C2) The Jewish Museum (Židovské Muzeum), founded in 1906 after the reconstruction of Josefov, includes the collectively managed Old Jewish Cemetery (p30), Ceremonial Hall, Maisel Synagogue, Pinkas Synagogue (p32), Spanish Synagogue (p32) and the Klaus Synagogue. The separately run Old-New Synagogue (p21) can be visited independently, or with the Jewish Museum. It's a fascinating grouping, but tourist prices are grossly inflated.
☎ 222 317 191 🖥 www.jewishmuseum.cz
✉ U starého hřbitova 3a, Josefov 💲 300/200Kč
🕐 9am-4.30pm Sun-Fri Nov-Mar; 9am-6pm Sun-Fri Apr-Oct; closed Jewish holidays Ⓜ Staroměstská
♿ only Old Jewish Cemetery, Maisel & Spanish synagogues

Lapidárium (6, C2) Fascinating examples of the mason's art gather in this gallery of 11th- to 19th-century Bohemian sculpture. Highlights

Reality at Army Museum

include the Kouřim Lions (the country's oldest stone sculpture), Jan Bendl's original equestrian statue of St Wenceslas, the flamboyant Krocín Fountain and several Charles Bridge statues. The stately bronzes of Hapsburg emperors and Marshal Radecký look rather forlorn in the last room.
☎ 233 375 636 🖥 www.nm.cz
✉ Fairgrounds (Výstaviště 422), Holešovice 💲 20/10Kč
🕐 noon-6pm Tue-Fri, 10am-6pm Sat-Sun
Ⓜ Nádraží Holešovice, then tram 5, 12, 17, 53 or 54 to Výstaviště ♿ good

Lobkowicz Palace (8, F1) The Lobkovický palác contains the National Museum exposition 'Monuments of the National Past', covering Czech history from settlement to the attempted democratic revolution of 1848. Eclectic artefacts on show include the moustachioed stone

Much Ado about Mucha

The Mucha Museum does a great job of presenting the life and times of Alfons Mucha, aided by the cooperation it receives from the celebrated artist's grandson and daughter-in-law in the guise of the Mucha Foundation. In fact, Mucha has become a very marketable commodity, as evidenced by the countless postcards, calendars, posters, mugs, playing cards and other touristy knick-knackery you'll see all around town. To appreciate some of his greatest work, take a tour of the **Municipal House** (p13).

head of a Celtic god and Napoleon's wine glass. The extensive notes will guide you through it all.

☎ 233 354 467
🖥 www.nm.cz
✉ Jiřská 3, Prague Castle, Hradčany 💲 40/20Kč 🕙 9am-5pm Tues-Sun Ⓜ Malostranská, Hradčanská ♿ limited

Mucha Museum (4, F4)

See the fine works of Art Nouveau master Alfons Mucha up close and personal. On show are some of his original theatrical posters, as well as his *Slav Epic* paintings and popular commercial posters such as The *Four Flowers*. Also here are photographs of Mucha's truly bohemian models and friends, including a trouser-less Paul Gauguin.

☎ 221 451 333
🖥 www.mucha.cz
✉ Panská 7, Nové Město
💲 120/60Kč 🕙 10am-6pm Ⓜ Můstek ♿ good

Old Royal Palace (8, D2)

Dating from 1135, the centrepiece of this grand

Gothic palace is the huge, vaulted Vladislav Hall; the balcony presents a superb vista over Prague. Off to one side is the Bohemian Chancellery, where the infamous Defenestration of Prague took place in 1618; the lucky defenestrates actually survived after landing in a vast pile of refuse.

☎ 224 373 368 (info centre) 🖥 www.hrad.cz
✉ Prague Castle, Hradčany 💲 Ticket A, 220/110Kč inc St Vitus Cathedral, Basilica of St George, Powder Tower & Golden Lane 🕙 9am-5pm Apr-Oct, 9am-4pm Nov-Mar Ⓜ Malostranská, then 22 or 23 to Pražskýhrad ♿ limited

Prague Castle Powder Tower (2, B3)

Edward Kelly and other alchemists sweated over their furnaces in this forbidding tower, vainly attempting to produce gold for Emperor Rudolf II (see the boxed text, Alchemical Kelly p36). Today there's a small display of antique

alchemical equipment on show, though unfortunately, labelling is Czech only.

☎ 224 373 368 (info centre) 🖥 www.hrad.cz
✉ Prague Castle, Hradčany 💲 Ticket A, 220/110Kč inc St Vitus Cathedral, Basilica of St George, Powder Tower & Golden Lane 🕙 9am-5pm Apr-Oct, 9am-4pm Nov-Mar Ⓜ Malostranská, then 22 or 23 to Pražskýhrad ♿ no access

Prague Jewellery Collection (4, B3)

Sumptuous necklaces, brooches, bangles and rings from the collections of the Museum of Decorative Arts (p20) are shown here, including some eye-catching baubles by the likes of Tiffany and Fabergé. Vintage evening gowns and exhibitions of contemporary Czech designers complete the collection.

☎ 221 451 333
✉ Cihelná 2b, Malá Strana 💲 60Kč
🕙 10am-6pm
Ⓜ Malostranská

GALLERIES

Convent of St Agnes (4, E1) Upstairs in the peaceful 1231 sanctum of Klášter Sv Anežky is an excellent National Gallery exhibition of Bohemian and Central European medieval art (13th-16th centuries); particularly striking are the altarpieces from the Cistercian monastery at Vyšší Brod. The ground-floor cloister has a tactile presentation of 12 casts of medieval sculptures with Braille plaques.
☎ 224 810 628
🖳 www.ngprague.cz
✉ Anežská 1, Josefov
💲 100/50Kč or 240/120Kč 2-day ticket inc Convent of St George & Sternberg Palace; free 1st Wed of month
🕓 10am-6pm Tue-Sun
Ⓜ Staroměstská, Náměstí Republiky ♿ limited

Convent of St George (8, D1) This old Benedictine convent building (Klášter Sv Jiří) has an exhibition of Bohemian art from early mannerist works to baroque, featuring artists such as Karel Škréta and Jan Kupecký. The top floor has impressive statuary.
☎ 257 320 536
🖳 www.ngprague.cz
✉ Jiřské náměstí 33, Prague Castle, Hradčany 💲 50/20Kč, or 240/120Kč 2-day ticket inc Sternberg Palace & Convent of St Agnes; free 1st Wed of month
🕓 10am-6pm Tue-Sun Ⓜ Malostranská, Hradčanská

Galerie MXM (4, A4) Hidden in an artistically unkempt courtyard, this private gallery is devoted to showcasing the creativity of younger artists, without any sign of stylistic restrictions. There's always something interesting (if not always palatable) on show.
☎ 257 311 198
✉ Nosticova 6, Malá Strana 💲 free 🕓 noon-6pm Tue-Sun Ⓜ Národní Třída, then tram 22, 23 or 57 to Újezd

Gallery of Surrealism (7, B1) This intriguing little gallery showcases the bizarre imaginings of Prague artist Viktor Safonkin (think Salvador Dali meets Hieronymus Bosch), with a rotating exhibition of weird and wonderful paintings. Prints of some of the works are for sale.
☎ 224 239 476
✉ Jachymová 2, Josefov 💲 free 🕓 10am-7pm Mon-Fri, noon-6pm Sat Ⓜ Staroměstská ♿ limited

House at the Golden Ring (7, D2) Much of the Renaissance Dům U zlatého prstenu is taken up by a fascinating exhibition of 20th-century art, with particular emphasis on the Czech passion for surrealism and just plain oddness. Highlights include Jan Zrzavý's bleak *Slagheaps in the Evening*, *Tyrš's Dream* by Antonín Landa, and Karel Malich's creepy wire sculpture, *Would You Like Another Beer?*
☎ 224 827 022
🖳 www.citygallery prague.cz ✉ Týnská 6, Staré Město 💲 60/30/120Kč 🕓 10am-6pm Tue-Sun Ⓜ Náměstí Republiky ♿ limited

Kinský Palace (7, D2) It was from the balcony of the late baroque Palác Kinských that Klement Gottwald proclaimed communist rule in 1948. Today, the National Gallery makes use of the palace as a temporary exhibition space for paintings and sculpture.

Something for Nothing
A healthy number of museums and galleries in Prague prescribe to the idea of public days, where entry fees are waived or reduced to a token amount. All National Gallery branches hold their open day on the first Wednesday of every month, and the National Museum and associated City of Prague museum have theirs on the first Monday and Thursday of each month, respectively. Freebies are noted in the relevant reviews. Children between six and 10 years of age often gain free admittance to exhibitions.

☎ 224 810 758
🖳 www.ngprague.cz
✉ Staroměstské náměstí 12, Staré Město $ 100/50Kč, free 1st Wed of month
🕐 10am-6pm Tue-Sun
Ⓜ Staroměstská, Můstek
♿ limited

Leica Gallery Prague (8, E1)
This ultra-modern gallery inside the Prague Castle compound plays host to wide-ranging and well-presented exhibitions of Czech and East European photography. There's also a very good specialist bookshop attached.
☎ 233 355 757
✉ Nejvyšší Purkrabství, Prague Castle, Hradčany $ 80/60Kč 🕐 10am-6pm Tue-Sun Ⓜ Malostranská ♿ good

Mánes Gallery (6, B4)
A 1930s incarnation of a gallery previously founded by artist Josef Mánes and friends in Kinský Gardens. It underwent a thorough refit during 2003, and is now a spanking new exhibition hall for contemporary Czech artists, with an on-site bookshop.
☎ 224 930 754
✉ Masarykovo nábřeží 250, Nové Město $ free
🕐 10am-6pm Tue-Sun
Ⓜ Karlovo Náměstí
♿ good

Sternberg Palace (2, C1)
Accessed by a passageway next to Archbishop's Palace, the baroque Šternberský palác serves as a branch of the National Gallery and has a small but remarkable collection of Old Masters, including works by El Greco, Piero della Francesca, Rembrandt and Rubens. Roman and Renaissance sculpture is also on show.
☎ 220 514 599
🖳 www.ngprague.cz
✉ Hradčanské náměstí 15, Hradčany $ 150/70Kč or 240/120Kč 2-day ticket inc Convent of St Agnes & Convent of St George; free 1st Wed of month 🕐 10am-6pm Tue-Sun Ⓜ Malostranská ♿ ground floor only

Strahov Gallery (2, B3)
Billed as one of Central Europe's most important monastic collections, the exhibits in the Strahovská obrazárna run the gamut of styles from Gothic and Rudolphine to rococo and baroque. The gallery also includes 19th-century Czech, and Italian and Flemish art.
✉ Strahovské nádvoří 1, Strahov $ 35/20Kč
🕐 9am-noon & 12.30-5pm Tue-Sun Ⓜ Malostranská, then tram 22 or 23 to Pohořelec

Summer Palace (5, A1)
The 16th-century Královský Leto hrádek is a prime example of Italian Renaissance architecture. Often referred to as the 'Belvedere', on occasions it is used to stage temporary exhibitions.
☎ 224 373 368 (info centre) 🖳 www.hrad.cz
✉ Prague Castle, Hradčany Ⓜ Malostranská, then tram 22 or 23 to Pražský hrad
♿ good

U prstenu Gallery (7, B4)
Commercial gallery mostly housing striking and innovative paintings by local artists; instalments usually change monthly. There are prints and lithographs for sale, display cases filled with jewellery and other interesting creations by Czech artisans.
☎ 224 222 864
🖳 www.uprstenu.cz
✉ Jilská 14, Staré Město
$ free 🕐 11am-7pm
Ⓜ Národní Třída

Another reality is seen at the Gallery of Surrealism

NOTABLE BUILDINGS & MONUMENTS

Dancing Building

(6, B4) The Dancing Building (Tančící dům) is a remarkably successful attempt at integrating avant-garde architecture into an old neighbourhood. Its fluid, just-melted form seems inexplicably natural. Behind the topmost metal and glass is one of Prague's best restaurants, **La Perle de Prague** (p70).
✉ Rašínovo nábřeží 80, Nové Město Ⓜ Karlovo Náměstí

Get your dancing shoes on to visit the Dancing Building

☎ 224 215 001
🖳 www.narodni-divadlo.cz ✉ Ovocný trh 1, Staré Město ☉ box office (Kolowrat Palace) 10am-6pm Mon-Fri, 10am-12.30pm & 3-6pm Sat-Sun Ⓜ Můstek ♿ good

František Palacký Monument (6, C4)

The best way to admire Stanislav Sucharda's bronze tribute to famed 19th-century historian Palacký, who helped lead the way during the Czech National Revival, is to stand beneath it and gaze up at the expressions on the monument's figures, particularly those behind the main man.
✉ Palackého náměstí, Nové Město Ⓜ Karlovo Náměstí ♿ good

Jan Hus Statue (7, C2)

Diverting pedestrian traffic in the middle of Old Town Square is the statuesque presence of Jan Hus, erected on 6 July 1915 on the 500th anniversary of the reformer's execution. The sombreness of Ladislav Šaloun's statue, which casts Hus alongside his followers

Estates Theatre (7, D3)

Prague's oldest theatre is one of its most beautiful neoclassical achievements. Opening as the Nostitz Theatre in 1783, it played host to the premiere of Mozart's *Don Giovanni* in 1787. Later renamed after the collective Bohemian nobility, the Stavovské Divadlo is now a principal Prague venue for operas, concerts and ballets, including the annual Opera Mozart festival.

Operation Anthropoid

One of the most daring and dangerous missions of WWII was 'Operation Anthropoid', the plan to 'liquidate' the brutal Nazi Reichsprotektor of Bohemia and Moravia, Reinhard Heydrich. British-trained Czechoslovak parachutists were dropped inside Czechoslovakia in December 1941 and on 27 May 1942 they ambushed Heydrich's staff car in the Libeň area of Prague. Heydrich died of his wounds in hospital, and a huge reward was offered for information on his killers. On 10 June, Nazi fury was directed at the village of Lidice (p31), which they completely destroyed, while on 18 June, the seven parachutists' hiding place in the Cathedral of Sts Cyril & Methodius was betrayed. Eight hundred German soldiers surrounded the building, but after a fierce gun fight, the parachutists shot themselves rather than be taken alive. The crypt is today kept as a shrine to their memory.

František Palacký Monument honours the historian

and a mother and child representing a reborn Czech nation, is relieved a little by encircling flowerbeds.

⊠ **Staroměstské náměstí, Staré Město**
🚊 17, 18, 51 or 54 to Staroměstská
♿ excellent

Klementinum (7, A3)

The massive Klementinum was a Jesuit college before becoming part of Charles University in 1773. From the inner courtyard, catch a tour of the grand baroque library – bookworms note that the pre-18th-century tomes are off-limits – and the 52m-high reconstructed Astronomical Tower.

☎ 603 231 241
⊠ **Mariánské náměstí, Staré Město** 💲 100/50Kč
🕐 noon-7pm Mon-Fri, 10am-7pm Sat-Sun
Ⓜ Staroměstská
♿ library only

Old Jewish Cemetery (7, B1)

Full of tilting sarcophagi and cascading tombstones, this nearly 600-year-old cemetery (Starý Židovský Hřbitov) is a surviving cornerstone of the Jewish community's long past, now part of the Jewish Museum. It has a rarefied, carefully preserved atmosphere (though large tour groups tend to disrupt it) and a Braille trail for the visually impaired.

☎ 222 317 191
🖥 **www.jewish museum.cz** ⊠ **Široká, Josefov** 💲 Jewish Museum 300/200Kč
🕐 9am-4.30pm Sun-Fri Nov-Mar; 9am-6pm Sun-Fri Apr-Oct; closed Jewish holidays Ⓜ Staroměstská
♿ good

Old Town Bridge Tower (4, C4)

The striking 14th-century Staroměstská mostecká věž was the point where the invading Swedes were repulsed in 1648, by a force of Catholic students and Jews. Today it houses a fairly humdrum collection of vintage musical instruments. The main point of interest though is the 138-step climb to the roof, for amazing views across the river.

⊠ **Karlův most, Staré Město** 💲 40/30Kč
🕐 10am-6pm
Ⓜ Staroměstská

Powder Tower (7, F3)

There are fine views from this 65m-high neo-Gothic tower (Prašná Brána), built in 1475 and used to store gunpowder in the 18th century, now with an appropriately sooty look and a photo exhibit on the Prague skyline. Be careful with the steep stairs up to the 1st-floor ticket office.

⊠ **Na příkopě, Staré Město** 💲 40/30Kč
🕐 10am-6pm (ticket sales end 5.30pm) Apr-Oct Ⓜ Náměstí Republiky

Students Memorial (4, D5)

Under the arches at Národní 16 is a wall plaque with the metal-frozen image of numerous hands clamouring for peace, inscribed with the date '17.11.89'. It commemorates the day students marching in remembrance of those killed during an anti-Nazi protest 50 years earlier were clubbed by police. Subsequent protests saw the end of the communist regime.

⊠ **Národní 16, Nové Město** Ⓜ Národní Třída
♿ excellent

TV Tower (6, D3)

This 216m tower (Televizní Věž) is the tallest, and possibly the ugliest thing in Prague. On a clear day you can see up to 100km away from the viewing deck. The exterior is graced by a series of giant babies with barcodes for faces. Far out.

☎ 267 005 778
🖥 **www.tower.cz**
⊠ **Mahlerovy sady 1, Žižkov** 💲 150/30Kč
🕐 11am-11.30pm
Ⓜ Jiřího z Poděbrad

PLACES OF WORSHIP

Basilica of St George (8, D2) Bazilika Sv Jiří might have a baroque facade but deep down it's still a 10th-century Romanesque building, almost austere after the richness of St Vitus (p10). There are remnants of frescoes, and the chapels of St Ludmila and St John of Nepomuk are splendid. Catch one of the concerts here. ☎ 224 373 368 (info centre) 🖳 www.hrad.cz ✉ Prague Castle, Hradčany 💲 Ticket A, 220/110Kč, inc St Vitus Cathedral, Old Royal Palace, Powder Tower & Golden Lane 🕑 9am-5pm Apr-Oct, 9am-4pm Nov-Mar Ⓜ Malostranská, Hradčanská

Cathedral of Sts Cyril & Methodius (6, B4) This baroque Orthodox church is where the parachutists involved in 'Operation Anthropoid' (see the boxed text, 'Operation Anthropoid' p29) – hid out and died, after it was stormed by Nazi troops. The crypt now houses the moving 'Memorial to the Heroes of the Heydrich Terror'. ☎ 224 916 100 ✉ Resslova, Nové Mésto 💲 50/20Kč 🕑 10am-5pm Tue-Sun Ⓜ Karlovo Náměstí 🖐 good

Church of Our Lady of the Snows (4, E5) It feels like it *could* snow from the frosty heights of this Gothic church (Kostel Panny Marie Sněžné). Its towering black and gold altar is the city's highest. The church's lovely front courtyard is accessed through the archway of the Austrian Cultural Institute. ✉ Jungmannovo náměstí 18, Nové Mésto 🕑 6.30am-7.15pm Ⓜ Můstek

Church of St Francis of Assisi (4, C3) Run by a Czech order of crusaders established in the 12th century, the interior is circled by alabaster saints and has a startling fresco of the *Last Judgement* by WL Reiner on its cupola. There are regular concerts featuring the second-oldest organ in Prague.

☎ concert box office 221 108 266 ✉ Křížovnické náměstí, Staré Město 💲 church free; concerts 390/350Kč 🕑 10am-1pm & 2-6pm Tue-Sat, concerts 9pm Apr-Oct Ⓜ Staro-městská

Church of St Michael (6, B4) Hidden in the hillside tangle of Kinský Gardens, this church (kostel sv Michala), an 18th-century wooden structure, was brought over from a Ukrainian village in pieces and reassembled on Petřín Hill. It's boarded up, but worth viewing; take a map, it's hard to find.

✉ Kinský Gardens, Petřín Hill, Smíchov Ⓜ Anděl

Church of the Most Sacred Heart of Our Lord (6, D4) You'll be impressed by the imagination of Slovenian architect Josip Plečník, who in 1932 managed to anchor what looks like a stone freighter with a clocktower for a wheelhouse in the middle of náměstí Jiřího z Poděbrad.

Josefov

Jews settled in Prague in the 10th century but in the 13th century were forced into a ghetto when Rome demanded separation of the Jewish and Christian populations. Also called Jewish Town, the ghetto existed until 1848, when enlightened Emperor Joseph II had its walls demolished. The new Jewish district was subsequently named Josefov after him and became an official entity of the city.

From 1893, city administrators spent two decades redesigning the area as an outdoor Art Nouveau showcase. During WWII, the Nazis were responsible for the deaths of three-quarters of the local Jewish community and, not long afterwards, the communist regime spurred the emigration of many thousands more. It's estimated that the current Prague community numbers 5000-6000 people.

✉ náměstí Jiřího z Poděbrad 19, Vinohrady ⏰ services 8am & 6pm Mon-Sat; 7am, 9am, 11am & 6pm Sun Ⓜ Jiřího z Poděbrad

Pinkas Synagogue (7, A1) Part of the Jewish Museum (p25), Pinkasova Synagóga was built in 1535 and reconstructed in the 1950s as a memorial to Jewish victims of the attempted Nazi genocide in Bohemia and Moravia. It contains the sobering sight of 77,297 names marked in a community and family context on its walls, and affecting drawings by children imprisoned in Terezín (p45).

☎ 222 317 191 💻 www.jewish museum.cz ✉ Široká 3, Josefov Ⓢ Jewish Museum 300/200Kč ⏰ 10am-4.30pm Sun-Fri Nov-Mar; 10am-6pm Sun-Fri Apr-Oct; closed Jewish holidays Ⓜ Staroměstská

Rotunda of the Holy Cross (4, C5) This 12th-century church (Kaple Sv Kříže) is one of the few Romanesque structures still standing in Prague and is one of the oldest buildings in the city. Its modest style comes as a relief after the soaring splendour of other local places of worship.
✉ cnr Konviktstá & Karoliny Světlé, Staré Město ⏰ services 6pm Tue, 5pm Sun Ⓜ Národní Třída

Spanish Synagogue (4, D2) Dating from 1868 and part of the Jewish Museum collective, this synagogue (Španělská Synagóga) has a Moorish interior swirling with gilt, polychrome and stucco motifs. There's an exhibition on Jewish history and concerts are held here.
☎ 222 317 191 💻 www.jewishmuseum .cz ✉ Vězeňská 1, Josefov Ⓢ Jewish Museum 300/200Kč ⏰ 10am-4.30pm Sun-Fri Nov-Mar; 10am-6pm Sun-Fri Apr-Oct; closed Jewish holidays Ⓜ Staroměstská

PARKS & GARDENS

Chotek Park (4, A1) Landscaped in 1833, Chotkovy sady stretches east of the Summer Palace, and is Prague's oldest public park. Usually devoid of humanity, the park allows luxurious views south down the Vltava, where the river's bridges obligingly line themselves up to make it into your photo.
✉ Chotkovy sady, Hradčany Ⓜ Malostranská ♿ good

Františkánská zahrada (4, E5) The garden of the former Franciscan Ursuline convent is now a neat, enclosed park, offering an oasis of greenery just a few steps away from the bustle of Wenceslas Square. Crowds of local office workers,

shoppers and skateboarders vie with tourists for seating space on the benches, but it's still a pleasant place to catch your breath.
✉ Jungmannovo náměstí, Nové Město ⏰ 7am-10pm mid-Apr to mid-Sep; 7am-8pm mid-Sep to mid-Oct; 8am-7pm mid-Oct to mid-Apr Ⓜ Můstek ♿ good

Garden on the Ramparts (8, D3) Apart from offering a spectacular vista, the finely manicured Zahrada Na valech lets you get close to the castle's exterior, with its sloping concrete buffers. A great place to perch on a retaining wall in the sun, though you'll find snap-happy people will clamber over you to have their photo

taken with Prague as their personal backdrop.
☎ 224 373 368 (info centre) 💻 www.hrad.cz ✉ Prague Castle, Hradčany ⏰ 10am-6pm Apr-Oct Ⓜ Malostranská ♿ good

Letná Gardens (6, B2) Letenské sady has giddy views of the city and river from the concrete deck around its gigantic, and slightly creaky metronome. The device was built on the spot where an equally gigantic statue of Stalin was hoisted in 1955, then demolished in 1962. There are a few summertime bars and communal seating areas where you can enjoy a beer or three under the trees.

✉ Letenské sady, Letná Ⓜ Malostranská, then tram 12 to Čechův most; Hradčanská, then tram 1, 8, 25, 26, 51 or 56 to Sparta ♿ approach park from northern side

Royal Garden (5, B1)

Originally planted in 1535, Královská zahrada grants a royal respite from the crowded arena of Prague Castle. Wander through groves of mature trees and past entrancing buildings like the Renaissance Ball-Game House and Summer Palace. If the fountain in front of the palace is flowing, you might get to hear why it's called the 'Singing Fountain'.
☎ 24 37 33 68 (info centre) 💻 www.hrad.cz ✉ Mariánské hradby, Hradčany ⏲ 10am-6pm Apr-Oct Ⓜ Malostranská, then tram 22 or 23 to Pražský hrad

Stromovka (6, C2)

The huge expanse of trees and clearings to the west of the Fairgrounds is sometimes called Royal Deer Park because of its use as a hunting preserve in the Middle Ages. With

Royal Gardens, where you'll hear the fountain singing

its quiet lanes, duck ponds and weeping willows, it's a lovely place to get away from the city crowds.
✉ Stromovka, Bubeneč Ⓜ Nádraží Holešovice, then tram 5, 12, 17, 53 or 54 to Výstaviště ♿ good

Vojan Park (4, A3) Once part of a Carmelite convent, this sleepy park (Vojanovy sady) is Prague's oldest, established in 1248, though it only became public in 1955. The old surrounding walls keep the area's noise out, but there's a small children's play area near the front entrance where you can create some. Dogs and bikes are not permitted.
✉ U lužického semináře, Malá Strana ⏲ 8am-7pm (to 5pm Nov-Mar)

Ⓜ Malostranská ♿ good

Vyšehrad Gardens (6, C4) The small, secluded parks of ancient Vyšehrad make for an excellent escape from the city. Do a circuit around the ramparts to find your preferred slice of solitude, whether it's the benches on the southern side overlooking the small boat harbour, or the grassy lea near the rotunda.
☎ 224 920 735 ✉ Soběslavova 2, Vyšehrad ⏲ dawn-dusk Ⓜ Vyšehrad ♿ good

Wallenstein Garden

(4, A2) This magnificent formal garden complex (Valdštejnská zahrada) was built in the early 17th century in baroque style. It's dominated by a grand loggia, adorned with scenes from the Trojan War. The statues around the park are copies; the originals were taken by the Swedes during the Thirty Years' War.
✉ Letenská, Malá Strana ⏲ 9am-6pm May-Sep; 10am-6pm Apr & Oct Ⓜ Malostranská ♿ good

Garden on the Ramparts on the walls of Prague Castle

SQUARES & STREETS

Celetná Ulice (7, D2) The name of this pedestrianised strip of pastel facades linking Old Town Square with náměstí Republiky derives from the word *caltnéři*, which referred to the street's 14th-century bakers of *calty* (buns). It's still occupied by commerce, but now has a cluster of upmarket jewellery, perfume and Bohemian crystal shops.

✉ Celetná ulice, Staré Město Ⓜ Náměstí Republiky Ⓖ excellent

Charles Square (6, C4) Prague's biggest square (Karlovo náměstí) was created in the mid-14th century and has been coloured in with parkland. New Town Hall is at its northern end, while the south has Charles University's baroque Faust House. Look east for the golden-silhouetted statues of St Ignatius Church.

✉ Karlovo náměstí, Nové Město Ⓜ Karlovo Náměstí Ⓖ excellent

Hradčanské Náměstí (5, A3) Prague Castle's 'front yard' is an attraction in its own right, a large paved space bordered by the architectural melange of the Archbishop's Palace and the very loud sgraffito of the Schwarzenberg Palace. The square's small park is punctured by Ferdinand Brokoff's plague column, marking the Black Death's death in 1679.

✉ Hradčanské náměstí, Hradčany Ⓜ Malostranská Ⓖ excellent

Jan Palach Square (7, A1) This modest concrete and grass patchwork (náměsti Jana Palacha) is dedicated to philosophy student Jan Palach, who set himself ablaze on 16 January 1969 in protest against the Warsaw Pact invasion of Prague. A death-mask plaque of Palach is attached to the Univerzity Karlovy faculty he attended across the road.

✉ náměstí Jana Palacha, Josefov Ⓜ Staroměstská Ⓖ excellent

Loretánské Náměstí (2, B2) This 18th-century plot was originally the forecourt for the enormous Černin Palace, current residence of the Foreign Ministry. On its eastern side is the spiritually significant Loreta (p18), and to the north is the oldest still-operational Capuchin Monastery in Bohemia.

✉ Loretánské náměstí, Hradčany Ⓜ Malostranská, then tram 22 or 23 to Pohořelec Ⓖ good

Lucerna Passage (4, E6) This extensive, and somewhat gloomy, Art-Nouveau labyrinth (Pasáž Lucerna) under

Golden Lane

Golden Lane (8, E1) is the atmospheric and usually extremely crowded little thoroughfare in the northeastern corner of Prague Castle, which came into existence sometime after 1484, when the erection of a new outer castle wall created a passageway between itself and the older Romanesque fortifications. Originally called Zlatnická ulička (Goldsmith's Lane) after resident goldsmith guild members, it was a mini-shanty town of tiny dwellings, which later evolved into 'houses' for castle artillerymen. Today a row of 11 much-restored houses remains, now functioning as souvenir shops, selling everything from crystals to reproduction armour. There's also an imaginative mock-up of a medieval torture chamber and a crossbow range. At one end is the White Tower, where the alchemist Edward Kelly was held (see p36), while at the other is the Daliborka tower, one-time gaol of the 15th-century knight Dalibor, whose fiddle-playing inspired Smetana's eponymous opera.

Lucerna Palace, is bordered by Wenceslas Square, Štěpánská, V Jámě and Vodičkova. There are numerous shops, restaurants and a music club, as well as an upside-down copy of the famous Wenceslas statue dangling outside Lucerna cinema, by artist David Černý.

✉ **Lucerna Passage, Nové Město** Ⓜ **Muzeum** ♿ **good**

Gather your winter fuel in Wenceslas Square

Malé Náměstí (7, C3)
Literally a 'Little Square', beautifully surrounded by baroque and neo-Renaissance facades, including the sgraffito-decorated VJ Rott building, and with a wrought-iron fountain at its centre. Unfortunately it's often choked with traffic moving between Old Town Square and Charles Bridge.

✉ **Malé náměstí, Staré Město** Ⓜ **Staroměstská** ♿ **good**

Malostranské Náměstí (5, C3) Much of Malá Strana's busiest square is taken up by a car park and the enormous perimeter of the baroque St Nicholas Church (p24), with the brooding concert venue of Liechtenstein Palace taking plenty of space too. There are some good bars, pubs and restaurants around the square.

✉ **Malostranské náměstí, Malá Strana** Ⓜ **Malostranská** ♿ **good**

Maltézské Náměstí (5, C4)
Duck down quiet Prokopská to this attractive square, named after the Knights of Malta who established a monastery nearby. Beyond the statue of St John the Baptist is a side-street glimpse of the Church of Our Lady Below the Chain.

✉ **Maltézské náměstí, Malá Strana** Ⓜ **Malostranská** ♿ **good**

Na Příkopě (7, E4)
Prague's part pedestrianised High Street, lined with fashion outlets, restaurants and shopping arcades, slants down from náměstí Republiky to the northern tip of Wenceslas Square. Glitzy Western-style malls and chainstores dominate the scene.

✉ **Na příkopě, Nové Město** Ⓜ **Můstek, Náměstí Republiky** ♿ **excellent**

Nerudova (5, B3) Final steep stretch of the Royal Way running west from Malostranské náměstí, with Renaissance facades and hordes of gift shops and restaurants eyeing tourists travelling to and from the base of the castle. Buildings of note include the emblematic house of St John of Nepomuk (No 18) and the Church of Our Lady of Unceasing Succour (No 24).

✉ **Nerudova, Malá Strana** Ⓜ **Malostranská** ♿ **limited**

Pařížská Třída (7, C1)
Outdoor cafes and upmarket shops mingle with stately Art Nouveau apartment buildings on tree-lined 'Parisian Avenue', which swishes from Old Town Square north to the Vltava.

✉ **Pařížská třída, Josefov** Ⓜ **Staroměstská** ♿ **excellent**

Wenceslas Square (4, E5) Prague's biggest and busiest square, Václavské náměstí is more of an elongated boulevard, lined with shops and restaurants, continually crowded, and dominated at its southern end by the National Museum (p15). In 1968 and 1969 it was the scene of protests against the Soviet invasion, and of celebrations in 1989 as the communist regime was finally kicked out.

✉ **Václavské náměstí, Nové Město** Ⓜ **Můstek, Muzeum** ♿ **good**

QUIRKY PRAGUE

John Lennon Wall (4, A4)

From Lennon's 1980 murder until the communists' 1989 downfall, this was where activists defied the anti-pop authorities by scribbling Beatles lyrics and personal refrains. Lennonova zed got whitewashed in 1998 but today it's once again a psychedelic mess of spray-painted names and well-worn peace slogans, now scrawled by tourists, in numerous languages.
✉ Velkopřevorské náměstí, Malá Strana
Ⓜ Malostranská
♿ good

John Lennon Wall, stunning tribute to a call for peace

Museum of the Infant Jesus of Prague (5, C4)

The Church of Our Lady Victorious is dedicated to the cult of the Infant Jesus, which began in 1628 when Polyxena, a Spanish noblewoman, presented a wax statue of the Child Jesus to the friars here. The Muzeum Pražského Jezulátka displays its wardrobe of embroidered cloaks, while the figure itself sits in the marble altar in the church.
☎ 257 533 646
🖥 www.karmel.at/prag-jesu ✉ Karmelitská 9, Malá Strana 💲 free
🕐 9.30am-5.30pm Mon-Sat Ⓜ Malostranská

Muzeum Miniatur (2, A3)

Anatoly Koněnko is a Siberian artist who produces the tiniest works possible, all the pieces are just about visible in this extraordinary museum.

His works to date include a painted train on a human hair, a ship on a mosquito wing, a 3.2mm high replica of the Eiffel Tower and the world's most miniscule book – 0.9x0.9mm, inscribed, on 30 pages, with Chekhov's *The Chameleon*, with illustrations.
☎ 233 352 371
✉ Strahovské nádvoří 10, Strahov 💲 40/20Kč
🕐 9am-5pm Ⓜ Malostranská, then tram 22 or 23 to Pohořelec

Alchemical Kelly

When Emperor Rudolf II made Prague the Imperial capital in 1583, the city experienced a Golden Age, in more ways than one. As well as his patronage of the arts and sciences, Rudolf was obsessed with alchemy, and was particularly pleased when the English magician Dr John Dee and his companion, the Irish alchemist Edward Kelly, arrived on his doorstep. Kelly began public demonstrations of his 'art', supposedly learnt from a mysterious tome and secret powders he had discovered in Wales. Rudolf was so impressed he knighted Kelly and installed him in the Powder Tower of Prague Castle to work on producing gold for the state. Unfortunately, Kelly's powers failed him and he was imprisoned in the White Tower in Golden Lane. He twice attempted to escape, breaking a leg each time, and died soon afterwards, taking his secrets with him.

PRAGUE FOR CHILDREN

Prague has a growing range of sights and activities appealing to children of all ages, from well-maintained playgrounds to street theatre, puppet shows, child-friendly museums and, of course, lots and lots of cash- and plastic-hungry stores filled to the brim with tempting kids' stuff to cart home with you. Czechs are generally a family-oriented lot and most hotels can accommodate children, usually at a discounted price. Unlike many European countries, you won't see many children out with their families in the evenings, or in restaurants, although an increasing number of eateries do offer child menus. Nearly all tourist sights and attractions have reduced child tariffs.

Dětský ostrov (4, A6)
Prague's smallest island (Children's Island) offers a leafy respite from the busy city streets, with a few swings, climbing frames and a sandpit to occupy toddlers, as well as a mini football pitch and netball court for older siblings. There are plenty of benches for the less energetic, and there's also a restaurant (p77) on the island.
✉ Dětský ostrov
Ⓜ Anděl ♿ good

Divadlo Spejbla a Hurvínka (6, B2) Famous theatre established in 1930 by Josef Skupa and named after his father-and-son marionette creations (Spejbl and Hurvínek, respectively), which have since figured prominently in many Czech childhoods. The puppet shows range from straight comedy/drama to material with a visually 'grotesque' bent that has adult appeal.
☎ 224 316 784
🖥 www.spejbl-hurvinek.cz ✉ Dejvická 38, Dejvice 💲 40Kč
🕑 box office 10am-2pm & 3-6pm Tue-Fri 1-5pm, Sat-Sun; performances

10am Tue-Fri, 2pm & 4.30pm Sat-Sun
Ⓜ Dejvická

Fairgrounds (6, C2) The Fairgrounds (Výstaviště) is a sprawling enclave of pavilions, theatres and amusement rides (particularly when one of Prague's major fairs is on). Theatre and concerts are held in the **Spiral Theatre** (p89) and **Goja Music Hall** (p88), while kids might enjoy the spectacle of the computer-conducted Křižík Fountain 'dancing' to music.
🖥 www.krizikovafontana.cz ✉ U Výstaviště, Holešovice 💲 amusement rides 15-40Kč
Ⓜ Nádraží Holešovice,

then tram 5, 12, 17, 53 or 54 to Výstaviště ♿ good

Laser Game Fun Centre (4, D5) Subterranean video-game arcade in the Palác Metro mall, with the usual racing, kickboxing and shoot 'em up diversions. There's also a 'laser-quest' game arena for more active fun.
☎ 224 221 188
✉ Národni 25, Nové Město 💲 laser game 149Kč, credit chips 10Kč each (most games cost 2 credits) 🕑 10am-midnight Ⓜ Národní Třída

Maze (5, A5) Mirror maze (Bludiště) atop Petřín Hill, where kids get to distort themselves with no lasting

Marionettes fascinate the oldies and amuse the kids

consequences. There's also a diorama called 'Battle Against Swedes on Charles Bridge in 1648', set at the end of the Thirty Years' War. ✉ Petřínské sady, Malá Strana $ 40/30Kč ⏱ 10am-7pm Apr-Aug; 10am-6pm Sep-Oct; 10am-5pm Sat-Sun Nov-Mar Ⓜ Národní Třída, then tram 22, 23 or 57 to Újezd, then funicular up hill

Museum of Marionette Culture (7, A1) Rooms filled with a multitude of authentic, colourfully dressed marionettes from the late 17th to early 19th centuries. Star attractions are the Czech figures Spejbl and Hurvínek (see above review). The museum is upstairs inside the courtyard. ☎ 222 220 928 ⌨ www.puppetart.com ✉ Karlova 12, Staré Město $ 100Kč ⏱ 10am-8pm Ⓜ Staroměstská

National Technical Museum (6, C2) If you have only a mild interest in science and technology, this museum will catch your eye. Steam trains, planes, vintage cars and motorbikes are on show, as well as exhibitions on astronomy, photography and acoustics, and a mock-up of a coalmine. ☎ 220 399 111 ⌨ www.ntm.cz ✉ Kostelní 42, Holešovice $ 70/30Kč, audio guide 50Kč ⏱ 9am-5pm Tue-Sun Ⓜ Hradčanská, then tram 1, 8, 25, 26, 51 or 56 to Letenské náměstí

Prague Zoo (6, B1) Still recovering from the 2002 flood at the time of research, the zoo is now up and running again. Some of the many residents include the endangered Przewalski's horses, lemurs, leopards, kangaroos and aardvarks. There's a range of special events, including talks and feedings. ☎ 296 112 111 ⌨ www.zoopraha.cz ✉ U Trojského zámku 3, Troja $ 60/30Kč ⏱ 9am-5pm Mar; 9am-6pm Apr-May & Sep-Oct; 9am-7pm Jun-Aug; 9am-4pm Nov-Feb Ⓜ Nádraží

Look cool in Mirror Maze

Holešovice, then bus 112 to Zoo Praha ♿ good

Public Transport Museum (6, A3) There's a truck-load of trams and buses on show here, dating from 1886 up to the present day. Climb onto some of the exhibits for a better look, and if that whets your appetite, jump on Nostalgic Tram No 91 for a tour round town (p46). ☎ 296 124 905 ✉ Patočkova 4, Střešovice $ 20Kč ⏱ 9am-5pm Sat-Sun & public holidays end Mar-mid-Nov Ⓜ Hradčanská, then tram 1, 8, 18, 56 or 57 to Vozovna Střešovice ♿ good

Toy Museum (8, F1) A sizeable collection of vintage toys, from 19th-century wooden dolls and tin train sets to plastic robots from the '60's. The top floor is dominated by Barbie, in all her costumes, accompanied by a clutch of Kens and other friends. ☎ 224 372 294 ✉ Jiřská 6, Prague Castle, Hradčany $ 40/20Kč ⏱ 9.30am-5.30pm Ⓜ Malostranská, Hradčanská

Kid Care
The turnover of babysitting agencies in Prague is often as high as the turnover of their charges, but a few worth contacting are: **Babysitting** (☎ 604 241 270; Rytířova 812, Praha 4), with English and German speaking staff; **Babysitting Praha** (☎ 602 885 074) with 24 hour care on weekends, charging from 80Kč/hr; and **Babysitting – Markéta Tomková;** (☎ 777 999 877; marketa@tcheque.cz), which has English and French speakers at hand.

Out & About

WALKING TOURS
Josefov

Josefov is Prague's old 'Jewish Town', which comprised a ghetto as far back as the 13th century, until reconstruction in the late 19th century. Start the walk at **Franz Kafka's birthplace (1)**, just off Old Town Square. Head north along Maiselova past the **Maisel Synagogue (2**; p25) to the **Renaissance High Synagogue (3)**; across the laneway is Prague's oldest and most important Jewish temple, the **Old-New Synagogue (4**; p25). Go west down U starého hřbitova alongside the **Old Jewish Cemetery (5**; p30), Europe's old-est. You'll pass Klaus Synagogue

Old Jewish Cemetery, Europe's oldest

and **Ceremonial Hall (6**; p25), the cemetery's former mortuary, before dog-legging north to Břehová. Turn left, then left again onto 17.listopadu to reach the **Museum of Decorative Arts (7**; p20). Cross the road to **Jan Palach Square (8**; p34), and stare down the massive **Rudolfinum (9)**. Re-cross 17.listopadu and go east along Široká to **Pinkas Synagogue (10**; p32), a memorial to Jews who died during WWII. Continue east and turn left on chic **Pařížská (11)** to grab a drink at one of the pavement cafe's. Just north of here, turn right on Bílkova and follow it through Josefov's engaging backstreets to Kozí. Go left, then right on U milosrdných, and left up Anežská to the medieval art collection in the **Convent of St Agnes (12**; p27).

distance	1.5km
duration	1½hr
▶ **start**	Ⓜ Staroměstská
● **end**	🚋 5, 8, 14 or 53 from Revoluční, cnr Dlouhá

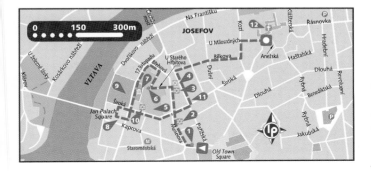

Royal Way

The Royal Way is the ancient coronation route to Prague Castle. Start from náměstí Republiky. First gaze in awe at the Art Nouveau splendour of the **Municipal House** (**1**; p13), then stroll under the **Powder Tower** (**2**; p30) and onto **Celetná** (**3**; p34). Admire the cubist **House of the Black Madonna** (**4**) before doubling back up Celetná and swinging north up Králodvorská, past the Art Nouveau-ish **Hotel Paříž** (**5**; p96) to Kotva. Turn left into Jakubská and walk down to **St James Church** (**6**), then cross Malá Štupartská and duck into Týn Court for a pick-me-up at **Ebel Coffee House** (**7**; p73). Walk out of the court's western end and go past the

Exuberant facade of Municipal House

northern door of **Týn Church** (**8**; p16) into Old Town Square (Staroměstské náměstí). Veer southwest to emerge into pastel-lined **Malé Náměstí** (**9**; p35). Bear left, then right into Karlova. Follow Karlova through the tourist crush and along the hulking **Klementinum** (**10**; p30) to Křižovnicka and **Charles Bridge** (**11**; p9). Cross the Vltava and head up Mostecká into the bustle of **Malostranské náměstí** (**12**; p35), where you'll be greeted by the baroque splendour of **St Nicholas** (**13**; p24). Cross to the square's northern side and turn left into **Nerudova** (**14**; p35), the steep road leading to the castle, cluttered with shops. Ease up the hill past beer halls and tearooms until reaching the driveway of your ultimate destination, **Prague Castle** (**15**; p8).

distance 3.5km
duration 1½-2hr
▶ **start** Ⓜ Náměstí Republiky
● **end** Ⓜ Malostranská; 🚊 12, 22, 23 or 57 from Malostranské náměstí

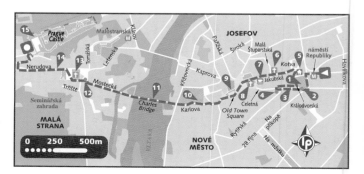

Vltava & Petřín Hill

Take your mark at Malostranská metro station. Head south down Klárov and turn right into Letenská for the manicured botany of **Wallenstein Garden** (**1**; p33). Back-track to Klárov and turn right down U lužického semináře. Poke your head into the sheltered confines of **Vojan Park** (**2**; p33) before continuing south to cross the small bridge under Charles Bridge. Straight ahead is Na Kampě, where you take one of the small lanes to the right and cross the canal into Velkopřevorské náměstí, site of the multicoloured **John Lennon Wall**

(**3**; p36). Return to Na Kampě and continue south to **C'est La Vie** (**4**; p66), where you can eat delicious seafood beside the river. Turn right on Říční. Go to the end, turn right on Újezd, then left on U lanové dráhy to either walk or catch the **funicular** (**5**) to the top of **Petřín Hill** (**6**; p23). On the hilltop, veer right along the Hunger Wall to climb Petřín Tower and groom yourself in the mirrors of the **Maze** (**7**; p37). Head north through the gardens to the impressive surrounds of **Strahov Monastery** (**8**; p17), and finish your walk with a glass of Czech wine at **Oživlé Dřevo** (**9**; p63).

distance 2.15km
duration 2hr
▶ **start** Ⓜ Malostranská
● **end** 🚊 22 or 23 from Keplerova, cnr Pohořelec

Strahov (above), Malá Strana (below)

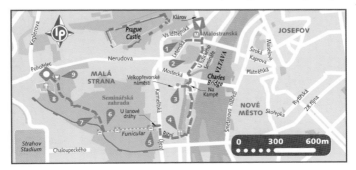

Wenceslas Square to Old Town Square

Begin on the **National Museum** steps (**1**; p15), from where you can see the entirety of Wenceslas Square stretching out before you. Cross the road to Josef Myslbek's statue of St Wenceslas (**2**), erected in 1912, and then walk down the square's western side to one of several entrances to the atmospheric **Lucerna Passage** (**3**; p34). Further north is the Melantrich Building (**4**) – President Havel announced communism's end from its balcony in 1989. Cross the square to the impressive facade of **Hotel Europa** (**5**), then continue north through the consumer chaos to the intersection rather hopefully called the 'Golden Cross' (**6**). To your right is the flashy shopping strip of **Na příkopě** (**7**; p35), but head left through the small arcade to Jungmannovo náměstí and the entrance to the lofty **Church of Our Lady of the Snows** (**8**; p31). Double back and then head north up crowded Na mustků to check out **Havelská Market** (**9**; p59). Further north on Melantrichova is the vegetarian **Country Life** (**10**; p72), great for a healthy, revitalising meal before taking the final plunge into **Old Town Square** (**11**; p11). You'll probably have to flail through a crowd in front of the **Astronomical Clock** (**12**; p14) to get to the square's centrepiece, the **Jan Hus Statue** (**13**; p29).

distance 1.5km
duration 1hr
▶ start Ⓜ Muzeum
⦿ end Ⓜ Staroměstská

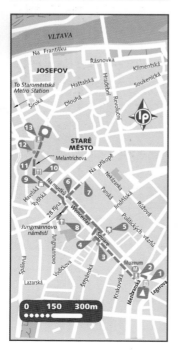

Astronomical Clock, Havelská Market

DAY TRIPS
Karlštejn (1, A3)

Karlštejn Castle's foundations were laid in 1348 by King/Emperor Charles IV, who used the crag-top edifice as a safe storehouse for the Imperial treasures. The castle's reputation for impregnability led Emperor Sigismund to deposit both the Bohemian and Imperial crown jewels here at the outbreak of the Hussite revolt, and the place was later used as a public records office. The castle was given a fresh medieval shape in the 1890s, and is now stormed by foreign armies of tourists most days; it's the most popular and best-preserved castle in the Czech Republic. Standard tours visit internal features like the **Knights' Hall**, decorated with coats-of-arms, the **Hall of Ancestors**, filled with 17th-century royal portraits, and the **Treasury**, where

INFORMATION

25km southwest of Prague

- Ⓜ Hlavní Nádraží, then local train (50min; 58Kč return) to Karlštejn, then a 20-25min walk to the castle through town or 10min horse and cart ride (150Kč per person). Note that some returning trains only go as far as Smíchovské Nádraží.
- ☎ 274 008 154
- 🖳 reservace@spusc.cz
- ⓘ ticket office in main courtyard
- ⌚ 9am-noon & 1-4pm Tue-Sun Apr & Oct; 9am-noon & 12.30-5pm Tue-Sun May-Jun & Sep; 9am-noon & 12.30-6pm Tue-Sun Jul & Aug; 9am-noon & 1-3pm Tue-Sun Nov-Mar (closed day after public holidays)
- Ⓢ 50min tour Route 1 200/100Kč, Route 2 (Chapel of the Holy Cross) 300/100Kč (Jul-Nov only; this route must be booked in advance by phone)

Karlštejn Castle, stormed by tourists

you can see replicas of the crown jewels, but it's the view from the outside that's most impressive.

If time permits, take a peep at the curious **Muzeum Betlémů** (9am-7pm Jul-Sep; 40Kč) down in the village with its collection of intricate Nativity scenes. The huge, mechanical 'Royal Crib of Karlštejn', with its 40 moving puppets, will make you come over all Christmassy.

View of well-preserved Karlštejn Castle

Kutná Hora (1, C2)

Kutná Hora grew from a silver-ore find in the late 13th century and soon acquired the prestige of being home to the Royal Mint and the king's

INFORMATION

70km southeast of Prague

- Kutná Hora main train station in Sedlec from Prague main train station (1hr; 90Kč return), then local train (8min; 8Kč one-way) to Kutná Hora město station, then 10-15min walk
- www.kutnohorsko.cz
- information centre, Palackého náměstí 377; ☎ 0327 512 378; 9am-6.30pm Mon-Fri, 9am-5pm Sat-Sun Apr-Oct; Mon-Fri 9am-5pm Nov-Mar
- ossuary: 8am-6pm Apr-Sep; 9am-noon & 1-5pm Oct; 9am-noon &1-4pm Nov-Mar; St Barbara's Church: 9am-5.30pm Tue-Sun May-Sep; 10-11.30am & 1-4pm Tue-Sun Apr & Oct; 10-11.30am & 2-3.30pm Tue-Sun Nov-Mar
- ossuary 30/20Kč; St Barbara's Church 30Kč

Gothic Ossuary, and yes, they're bones

residence, making it the most important place in Bohemia and one of Europe's power centres. All that changed when the silver ran out several centuries later, and Kutná Hora's decline was only compounded by the Thirty Years' War. Nowadays it's a mixture of often-striking streets, churches and assorted facades which contributed to it being World Heritage Listed by Unesco in 1996, and the slow pace and low-cost facilities of a small town.

The settlement has an attractive pastel-painted central square, Palackého náměstí, where the tourist infrastructure congregates. You'll find the information centre, taxis and cafes here. To the south-west are the magnificent Gothic spires of **St Barbara's Church** (Chrám sv Barbory), begun in 1380 but only finished in the late 19th century; set aside time to simply stare up at the decorative ceiling and to peruse the lovely surrounding hillsides.

Northeast of the centre, in the suburb of Sedlec, is the gruesomely fascinating handiwork of the ossuary in the **Chapel of All Saints**. The chapel became a skeletal repository in the 14th century, after plague overburdened the adjacent cemetery. František Rint, a Czech woodcarver, was responsible for arranging the myriad bones in their current stylised formations, which include crosses, chalices, a coat of arms, and a chandelier made of every bone in the human body. Local buses or taxis cover the 2km from the main square to Sedlec.

Terezín (1, A1)

The massive structure of Terezín, which includes 4km of walls and moats, was built in 1780 by Emperor Joseph II as defensive ramparts against Prussian aggression, and was subsequently used as a garrison post and then a prisoner-of-war camp during WWI. In 1940, the Lesser Fortress became a Gestapo prison, and by the end of 1941 the Main Fortress had been turned into a Nazi transit camp that eventually saw the passage of over 150,000 Jews as they were being transported to extermination camps. At the peak of its use for this horrific purpose, Terezín held 60,000 people in a space originally meant for 5000; 35,000 Jews imprisoned here died from disease, starvation or suicide.

Inside the monumental Main Fortress, on Komenského, is the **Museum of the Ghetto**, which documents the development of Nazism and the way Jewish people tried to conduct their lives in Terezín via videos, photographs, personal letters and artwork; pictures drawn by some of the many children incarcerated in Terezín are also on display at the Pinkas Synagogue (see p25) in Prague. There's a second branch of this

INFORMATION

50km northwest of Prague

Ⓜ Florenc, then bus from Florenc bus station (72Kč)

🖳 www.pamatnik-terezin.cz

ⓘ information centre in town hall, náměstí České armády; ☎ 0416 782 616

🕙 Museum of the Ghetto & Magdeburg Barracks: 9am-6pm Apr-Sep, 9am-5.30pm Oct-Mar; Crematorium: 10am-5pm Sun-Fri Apr-Nov; Lesser Fortress: 8am-6pm Apr-Sep, 8am-4.30pm Oct-Mar

$ combined ticket to museum/ barracks, crematorium & Lesser Fortress 160/120Kč; individual sites 140/110Kč

Main gate of chilling Lesser Fortress

Imagine the horror in Lesser Fortress

museum at the corner of Tyršova and Vodárenská in the former **Magdeburg Barracks**, while 100m south of the fortress walls is the **Crematorium**, located in the Jewish cemetery. To the east of the Main Fortress is the **Lesser Fortress**, a challenging place to visit with its chilling remnants of barracks, cells and morgues. You can see it via a self-guided tour.

ORGANISED TOURS

If you've had enough of organising yourself, let someone else do it for you. There are many companies in Prague offering tours of the city using every imaginable form of transport, including your own feet, though there's not a lot of difference between the tours offered by the larger operators.

City Walks Runs a long list of unique tours, including the 'Ghost Trail', the 'Literary Pub Tour' and the 'Revolution Walk', recalling the events of 1968 and 1989. It also offers bike and scooter tours, while the six-hour 'Ultimate Tour' - by tram, boat and on foot - gives a comprehensive overview of the city. Free refreshments and mementoes on some trips.
☎ 222 244 531 🖳 www .praguewalkingtours.com ✉ meeting point under Astronomical Clock, Staré Město 💲 from 300/250Kč adult/child for 1½/2hr walk; 6hr Ultimate Tour 1000Kč; tickets sold on the spot 🕑 vary

George's Guided Walks Private guide service, run by the eponymous George, who will meet you at your hotel or anywhere else that's convenient. Tours include the 'Communism Walk' and 'Prague Terrible' if you fancy a stroll on the dark side of the city. Money back guarantee if not completely satisfied!
☎ 607 820 158 🖳 www.prague master.com 💲 200-400Kč 🕑 vary

Nostalgic Tram no 91 (4, D5) There are a several tramcars, made between 1908 and 1942, navigating a special sightseeing run called nostalgic tramline No 91. Trams depart from the Střešovice depot beside the Transport Museum (p38) and wind their way past Prague Castle, through Malá Strana, across Wenceslas Square and up to the Fairgrounds and back.
☎ 233 343 349 ✉ Patočkova 4, Střešovice 💲 25/10Kč 🕑 12-6pm on the hour Sat, Sun & public hols Apr to mid-Nov

Oldtimer 'History Trip' (7, D4) Take a history-slanted spin on the cobbled streets in either a vintage Praga Piccola or a just-as-vintage Praga Alfa; don't forget your straw boater and bring a parasol to twirl casually at onlookers.
☎ 607 112 559 🖳 www.historytrip.cz ✉ cars stationed at various locations 💲 40min tour: 800Kč 1-2-person car, 1200Kč 3-6-person car; rates for longer trips vary 🕑 depart when commissioned

Prague Sightseeing Tours (3, B12) See sights by bus, boat or on foot. The extensive 3½hr 'grand' coach/walking tour departs twice daily in summer, while day-trips run to places such as Karlovy Vary, Karlštejn and Kutná Hora. Tours depart from náměstí Republiky, where there's a ticket kiosk.
☎ 222 314 661 🖳 www.pstours.cz ✉ Klimentská 52, Nové Město 💲 3hr walking tour 350Kč, 3½hr bus/walking tour 620/520Kč, 2hr cruise with lunch 750/650Kč 🕑 vary

Praha Bike (3, C8) Jump on a bike for a two or three hour guided cycle through the city, or an easy evening peddle through the parks. Trips outside Prague can also be arranged, and helmets, safety locks and maps are provided. Bikes are available for private rental too.
☎ 732 388 880 🖳 www.prahabike.cz ✉ Dlouhá 24, Staré Město 💲 2hr city ride/park ride 420Kč, 3hr city ride 460Kč 🕑 11.30am, 2.30pm & 6pm May-Sep, 2.30pm Mar-Apr & Oct

Wittmann Tours (3, K12) Jewish guide service offering bus and walking tours of sights of Jewish interest in and around Prague. Trips further afield include the concentration camps of Auschwitz and Mauthausen and individually designed tours can also be arranged.
☎ 222 252 472 🖳 www.wittmann -tours.com ✉ Mánesova 8, Nové Město 💲 from 400Kč for 2hr walking tour; from US$35/hr for private guided tours

Shopping

A growing entrepreneurial spirit is delivering some unique Czech commodities into Prague's marketplace. Beautiful standards such as Bohemian crystal, Czech garnets and traditional ceramics are mixing it with some inspired home-grown fashions, music, decorative glassware and wines. With the array of often excellent, and reasonably priced, locally produced goods swelling all the time, you'll probably find yourself sorely tempted to loosen the purse strings at every turn.

Shopping Areas

The centre's single biggest, and most exhausting, retail zone is **Wenceslas Square** (4, E5), with the perimeter crammed purse-to-wallet with browsing visitors, and Czechs making beelines for their favourite stores. You can find pretty much everything here, from high fashion and music megastores to run-of-the-mill department stores and gigantic book emporia. Many intriguing outlets are hidden in side-alleys such as **Lucerna Passage** (4, E6).

Mannequin headless in Saska street

The other main shopping drag is the extended thoroughfare comprising **Národní třída** (4, C5), **28.října** (4, E4) and **Na příkopě** (4, F4). Most of the big shops are concentrated along Na příkopě, which is studded with flashy Western-style malls and a variety of upmarket stores. Elsewhere, **Pařižská** (4, D3) is the place to go for international designer chic (sadly, at international prices), while the winding streets between the Old Town Square and Charles Bridge are regularly thronged with tourists perusing the puppets, Che Guevara T-shirts and Russian dolls which spill out from numerous tacky souvenir shops.

Opening Hours

Local businesses usually open 8-10am and close 5-7pm weekdays; count on Saturday hours being at least 10am-2pm and on many places being closed Sunday. That said, hours vary a lot: smaller outlets prefer later starts and earlier finishes to the bigger places; shops operate for an hour or two more during warmer months; and businesses in central Prague generally keep longer hours than their suburban counterparts.

Department stores tend to be open 9am-8pm weekdays, and from 10am-6pm on weekends.

DEPARTMENT STORES & SHOPPING MALLS

Černá Růže (7, E4) The 'House of the Black Rose' is a 3-floor shopping mall offering a truly random selection of retail outlets. You can pick up a few bottles of fine wine, Bohemian crystal goblets, baggy surfer pants, a skateboard and even some ladies' wigs if the mood strikes you. There are also a few cafes and a pizzeria.
✉ Na příkopě 12, Nové Město ☿ 9am-8pm Mon-Fri, 9am-7pm Sat, 11am-7pm Sun
Ⓜ Můstek

Dům Značkové Módy (4, F6) The busiest part of DZM is the flashy ground-floor perfumery, where local lads and lasses spray the air with the scents of Jean Paul Gaultier, Elizabeth Arden and Hugo Boss. Upstairs there are a few floors of generally unexciting men's and women's clothes, which see rather less traffic.
✉ Vaclavské náměstí 58, Nové Město ☿ 9am-9pm
Ⓜ Muzeum

Kotva (7, F1) Huge, ugly, angular, and rather brown mall with five floors of varied goods, from dated clothing ranges to electronics, sports equipment, toys, furniture, china and glass. There's also a pharmacy and a tax-free service on the ground floor.
☎ 224 801 111
✉ náměstí Republiky 8
☿ 9am-8pm Mon-Fri, 10am-7pm Sat, 10am-6pm Sun Ⓜ Náměstí Republiky

Slovanský Dům (7, F3) Prague's glitziest shopping mall, housing a 10-screen cinema and a nightclub, plus numerous upmarket fashion outlets and restaurants. There's a pleasant open courtyard at the back with a beer garden for the tired and thirsty and more shops for serial spenders.
☎ 221 451 400
🖥 www.slovanskydum .cz ✉ Na příkopě 22, Nové Město ☿ 10am-8pm Ⓜ Náměstí Republiky

Tesco (4, D5) This bustling, multistorey maze of consumerism will leave even the hardiest shopperholic feeling dazed and confused. The ground floor takeaway

Tesco's bright invitation

food section draws a shuffling queue, while other floors display everything from baby wear to electrical equipment. There's also a cafe and a huge, and very busy, basement supermarket.
☎ 222 003 111
✉ Národní 26, Nové Město ☿ 8am-9pm Mon-Fri, 9am-8pm Sat, 10am-8pm Sun
Ⓜ Národní Třída

Vinohradský Pavilion (3, C1) Housed in an imposing 19th-century market hall, this trendy mall, which calls itself 'the jewel of Prague shopping centres', has four floors of brand-name fashions such as Kenzo and Hilfiger, plus electronics, jewellery and household goods. Also here is the regulation basement supermarket and cafe.
☎ 222 097 111
✉ Vinohradská 50, Vinohrady ☿ 9.30am-9pm Mon-Sat, 10am-8pm Sun Ⓜ Jiřho z Poděbrad

A Christmas decorated Tesco Store in Prague New Town

CLOTHING & ACCESSORIES

Boheme (7, C1) Opened in 2002, this trendy clothing store showcases the designs of Hana Stocklassa and her associates, with collections of knitwear, leather and suede togs for women. Suede skirts, linen blouses and sweaters seem to be the stock in trade, and there's also a range of jewellery.
☎ 224 813 840
⌨ www.boheme.cz
✉ Dušní 8, Nové Město
☽ 10am-7pm Mon-Fri, 11am-4pm Sat
Ⓜ Staroměstská

Dunhill (7, C1) Nothing to wear to that social event of the season? Then you'll probably find what you need in this upmarket British fashion house, with its wide selection of men's casual and formal wear. While you're there you can also take a look through their watches, wallets and fragrances.
✉ Pařižská 14, Josefov

☽ 10am-7pm Mon-Fri, 11am-5pm Sat-Sun
Ⓜ Staroměstská

Helena Fejková Gallery (4, F5) Kit yourself out in the latest Czech fashions at this boutique and showroom. Contemporary men's and women's clothing and accessories by Prague designer Helena Fejková and others are on display, and private fashion shows can be arranged. There's another outlet in the Kotva shopping mall (p48).
☎ 224 211 514
⌨ www.helenafejkova.cz
✉ Lucerna Passage, Štěpánská 61, Nové Město
☽ 10am-7pm Mon-Fri, 10am-3pm Sat
Ⓜ Muzeum

Ivana Follová (7, D2) Prague designer Ivana Follová specialises in hand-painted silk dresses, many of which can be seen at this boutique in Ungelt. Only

Fleischmanova shop

natural materials are used in her colourful creations, and accessories, such as handmade glass beads, are also available.
☎ 224 895 460
⌨ www.ifart.cz ✉ Týn Court 1, Staré Město
☽ 10am-6pm
Ⓜ Náměstí Republkiy

Jackpot & Cottonfield (7, E4) Danish style at upmarket Czech prices. Cottonfield is for the men, with an array of casual cords,

CLOTHING & SHOE SIZES

Women's Clothing

Aust/UK	8	10	12	14	16	18
Europe	36	38	40	42	44	46
Japan	5	7	9	11	13	15
USA	6	8	10	12	14	16

Women's Shoes

Aust/USA	5	6	7	8	9	10
Europe	35	36	37	38	39	40
France only	35	36	38	39	40	42
Japan	22	23	24	25	26	27
UK	3½	4½	5½	6½	7½	8½

Men's Clothing

Aust	92	96	100	104	108	112
Europe	46	48	50	52	54	56

Japan	S	M	M		L	
UK/USA	35	36	37	38	39	40

Men's Shirts (Collar Sizes)

Aust/Japan	38	39	40	41	42	43
Europe	38	39	40	41	42	43
UK/USA	15	15½	16	16½	17	17½

Men's Shoes

Aust/UK	7	8	9	10	11	12
Europe	41	42	43	44½	46	47
Japan	26	27	27.5	28	29	30
USA	7½	8½	9½	10½	11½	12½

Measurements approximate only; try before you buy.

knits and checked shirts, while Jackpot is for the women, with an assortment of florid styles designed with bohemian wannabes in mind.

☎ 224 213 744 ✉ Na příkopě 13, Nové Město ⏲ 10am-8pm Mon-Sat, 11am-7pm Sun Ⓜ Můstek

Karpet (5, B3) The ground floor of the former abode of St John of Nepomuk, the Czech patron saint, is now occupied by a milliner's shop, selling all kinds of locally made hats, caps, berets and other assorted headgear for the gentleman about town.

✉ Nerudova 18, Malá Strana ⏲ 8am-8pm Ⓜ Malostranská

Marks & Spencer (7, E3) British high-street fashion comes to Prague, with two floors of men's and women's clothing in M&S's traditional smart-casual and more formal designs. There's also a small range of kids' clothes

and a toiletries section.

☎ 224 235 735 ✉ Na příkopě 19, Nové Město ⏲ 9.30am-8pm Mon-Fri, 10am-7pm Sat, 10.30am-7pm Sun Ⓜ Můstek

Promod (4, E4) Big, bright and bold women's wear store – one of five branches in Prague – offering two floors of youthful and con-temporary Czech fashion for the stylish girl-about-town. It also has a selection of shoes, handbags and other assorted accessories.

☎ 296 327 701 🖳 www.promod.com ✉ Václavské náměstí 2, Nové Město ⏲ 10am-9pm Mon-Sat, noon-7pm Sun Ⓜ Můstek

Salvatore Ferragamo (7, C1) Treat your feet to Florence's finest footwear in this modish boutique, with elegant styles for both men and women. Pricey accessories such as belts and bags can also be had.

✉ Pařižská 10, Josefov

Shop in Pařižská street

⏲ 10am-7pm Mon-Fri, 10am-6pm Sat Ⓜ Staroměstská

Senior Bazar (4, G4) Popular second-hand clothes outlet, with plenty of bargains to be found amongst the racks. Vintage dresses, suits, jeans and more recent castaways are all in search of new homes.

☎ 224 235 068 ✉ Senovážné náměstí 18, Nové Město ⏲ Mon-Fri 9am-5pm Ⓜ Náměstí Republiky

Sydney Store (4, G4) If you find yourself in need of an Australian bush-hat or wax jacket whilst in Prague, this is the place to come. There's also a range of more conventional clothes from Downunder, of the check shirt and chinos variety, as well as the odd pair of hiking boots and a small selection of wine and cigars.

☎ 224 398 288 🖳 www.kakaduaustralia .cz ✉ Senovážné náměstí 26, Nové Město ⏲ Mon-Fri 9am-7pm, Sat 9am-2pm Ⓜ Náměstí Republiky

Taxing Times

As a foreigner, it's possible to rid yourself of up to 16% value-added tax (VAT) on certain upmarket commodities by doing the following:

Buy goods worth at least 1000Kč from a shop displaying a 'Tax Free Shopping' sign; when handing over your cash/plastic, ask for a tax-free shopping cheque (to be filled out in the shop with your name and address); leave the Czech Republic within 30 days from date of purchase and get the cheque stamped by Czech customs; finally, head for one of the payment points listed on the ubiquitous *Where to Shop Tax Free – Prague* brochures within six weeks of purchase and get your refund.

JEWELLERY

Detail (4, E2) One of seven stores in Prague selling innovative and contemporary silver jewellery, at reasonable prices. Other oddments on offer include 'ethnic' carvings and textiles.
☎ 222 329 481
✉ Haštalská 8, Josefov
🕙 10am-6pm
Ⓜ Náměstí Republiky

Fabergé (7, C1) The jewellers to the Tsars certainly know how to put on the most mesmerising displays. This gorgeously stocked store has their trademark Easter egg pendants, as well as a sparkly array of rings, cufflinks, brooches and other top-end ornaments.
☎ 222 323 639
✉ Pařížská 15, Josefov
🕙 10am-8pm
Ⓜ Staroměstská

Galerie Vlasta (7, C2) This small boutique showcases the delicate gold and silver wire jewellery of award-winning contemporary Czech designer Vlasta Wasserbaurová. There's a range of highly distinctive net-like brooches, necklaces and earrings on display.
☎ 222 318 119 ✉ Staroměstské náměstí 5, Staré Město 🕙 10am-6pm Mon-Fri, 10am-1pm Sat Ⓜ Staroměstská

Granát Turnov (4, E2) Reputedly the biggest creator of Bohemian garnet jewellery, Granát Turnov offers silver and gold rings, brooches, cufflinks and necklaces showing off the

Garnet Therapy

The blood-red rock that you'll see dangling off the wrists, necks, ears and the odd eyebrow of the city's human traffic is more than likely one of the more colourful versions of the Czech garnet (český granát), a popular urban accessory and an even more popular tourist purchase. Garnets aren't always red – some are almost colourless and others are black, while the scarce green garnet is much sought-after. According to traditional rumours (often embellished by retailers) the gemstone consistently wields its mystical powers to replace sadness with joy.

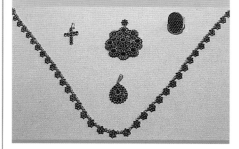

unique blood-red stones. Pearl and diamond jewellery is also on sale, as well as expensive ornaments comprising the dark-green, semi-precious stone *vltavín*.
☎ 222 315 612
🖥 www.granat-cz.com
✉ Dlouhá 30, Josefov
🕙 10am-6pm Mon-Sat, 10am-1pm Sun
Ⓜ Náměstí Republiky

Prague Diamond (7, B1) Allegedly the largest jewellery shop in Central Europe, Prague Diamond specialises in Marilyn Monroe's best friend, with loose and mounted stones in a wide variety of sizes and hues on offer. You can also watch a

short film about diamonds and visit the on-site workshop.
☎ 224 811 011
✉ Maiselova 21, Josefov 🕙 9am-8pm Ⓜ Staroměstská

U České orlice (7, E2) Elegant traditional Czech jewellery, including lots of garnets and chunky amber, as well as more restrained pieces in gold and silver. Exquisite, hand-painted porcelain and other *objets d'art* fill out the shop.
☎ 224 228 544
✉ Celetná 30, Staré Město 🕙 10am-8pm Ⓜ Náměstí Republkiy

ARTS & CRAFTS

Art Décoratif (7, F2)
Beautiful shop dealing in Czech-made reproductions of fine Art Nouveau and Art Deco glassware, jewellery and fabrics, including some stunning vases and bowls. It's also an outlet for the gorgeously delicate glass creations by Jarmila Plockova, grand-daughter of Alfons Mucha, who has used elements of his paintings in her work.
☎ 220 002 350 ⊠ U Obecního domu, Staré Město ⊗ 10am-8pm Ⓜ Náměstí Republiky

Celetná Crystal (7, E2)
This vast, sparkling emporium has a dazzling range of traditional and contemporary cut crystal laid out on three floors, so whether it's martini glasses, crystal pineapples, chandeliers or any other glassy luxury you're looking for, you are most likely to find it here. Bohemian porcelain and garnet and amber jewellery are there to tempt you.
☎ 222 324 022 ⊒ www .czechcrystal.com

⊠ Celetná 15, Staré Město ⊗ 10am-10pm Ⓜ Náměstí Republiky

Galerie Chez Annamarie (4, A3) Paintings, sculptures, ceramics and lithographs by contemporary Czech artists are on display and for sale in this interesting if slightly pricey gallery.
☎ 257 530 794 ⊒ www.annamarie.cz ⊠ Mostecká 14, Malá Strana ⊗ 11am-7pm Ⓜ Malostranská

Galerie Pyramida (4, C5) Commercial gallery with wonderfully original samples of art, sculpture and striking glass creations by contemporary Czech artists on display. This being Prague, the element of Surrealism is never far away, and many pieces have more than a touch of the psychedelic fantasy about them.
☎ 224 213 1 17 ⊠ Národní 11, Nové Město ⊗ 10.30am-7pm Ⓜ Národní Třída

Arty Galerie Pyramida

Kubista (7, E2)
Appropriately located in the Cubist House of the Black Virgin, this shop specialises in limited-edition reproductions of distinctive Cubist ceramics and furniture. They also have a few original pieces, including the kind of chairs Braque might have sat on, for serious collectors with serious cash.
☎ 224 236 378 ⊒ www.kubista.cz ⊠ Ovocný trh 19, Staré Město ⊗ 10am-6pm Ⓜ Náměstí Republiky

Manufactura (7, C3)
Multibranch store selling a huge array of traditional Czech handicrafts, including the ubiquitous wooden toys, scented soaps (cream and vanilla seem very popular), beeswax candles, ceramics, linen, ironwork and colourful, hand-painted *kraslice* (Easter eggs), which carry a variety of designs from around the country.
☎ 221 632 4 80 ⊒ www.manufactura.biz ⊠ Melantrichova 17,

Easter eggs at Manufactura for a truly festive look

Staré Město ✆ 10am-7pm Mon-Thu, 10am-7.30pm Fri-Sun Ⓜ Můstek

Moser (7, C3) One of the most well-respected Bohemian glassmakers, Moser was founded in Karlovy Vary in 1857 and is famous for its rich and flamboyant designs. On display are numerous examples of their trademark engraved glassware, both functional and purely decorative.
☎ 221 611 520 ⌨ www .moser-glass.com
✉ Malé náměstí 11,

Staré Město ✆ 10am-8pm Ⓜ Staroměstska

Rott Crystal (7, B3) Rott's fabulous sgraffito-covered 'shopfront' depicts tools and artisans from its previous incarnation when it was a steel company. Today, it houses innumerable pieces of garnet jewellery, china and glasswork. But Rott is known best for its stock of local and imported crystal: typically exquisite examples of traditional and modern Bohemian glitter away on the upper floors.
☎ 224 229 529

Cashpi Crystal shop

✉ Malé náměstí 3, Staré Město
✆ 10am-10pm
Ⓜ Staroměstská

ANTIQUES & BRIC-A-BRAC

Alma (7, A2) Alma specialises in Art Deco and Art Nouveau, and also has a wide selection of rather twee porcelain and lacy items. They also have a veritable army of scary looking dolls, stuffy furniture and glassware.
☎ 222 325 865
✉ Valentinská 7, Staré Město ✆ 10am-6pm
Ⓜ Staroměstská

Antik v Dlouhé (4, F2) Those with some spare time on their hands might enjoy a rummage through the 19th-century clutter in this curiosity shop. Amongst the junk there's some wonderful ceramics, jewellery and paintings, as well as the odd teddy bear, chandelier and mantle clock.
☎ 224 826 347
✉ Dlouhá 37, Josefov
✆ 10am-6pm Mon-

Fri, 10am-3pm Sat
Ⓜ Náměstí Republiky

Antique Ahasver (5, C4) This little shop is one big jumble of old lace – lots and lots of lace, everything from doilies to tablecloths. There's also a good collection of vintage dresses and the odd bits of jewellery and assorted knick-knacks.
☎ 257 531 404
✉ Prokopská 3, Malá Strana ✆ 11am-6pm Tue-Sun Ⓜ Malo-stranská, then tram 12, 22 or 57

Antique Music Instruments (2, B2) It might not get the prize for Prague's most inventive shop name, but this place is a real treasure trove of vintage stringed instruments. There's an interesting stock of

antique violins, violas and cellos dating from the 18th century up to the mid-20th century, as well as bows, cases and other musical accessories.
☎ 233 353 779
✉ Pohořelec 9, Hradčany ✆ 9am-6pm
Ⓜ Malostranská, then tram 22 or 23 to Pohořelec

Treasures in Bric à Brac

Art Deco (5, B3) All things '30s are the rage in this engaging, if tiny, boutique. There's lots of silver and glass on display, as well as some fashionable jewellery, both original and reproduction, and stunning Czech glass and porcelain from the Jazz Age.
☎ 257 535 801
✉ Jánský vršek 8, Malá Strana ☯ 2-7pm
Ⓜ Malostranská, then tram 12, 22 or 57 to Malostranské náměstí

Art Deco Galerie (7, C3) Unrelated to the above shop, this place has a larger selection of 1920s and '30s style, including some striking dresses and hats. China, glass and jewellery litter the store, along with knick-knacks such as cigarette cases of the sort Hercule Poirot might have used.
☎ 224 223 076
✉ Michalská 21, Staré Město ☯ 2-7pm Mon-Fri
Ⓜ Můstek

Bric à Brac (7, D2) Shop two of a two-shop franchise, with a jumble of eclectic antique oddments to please even the most demanding knick-knack aficionado, including typewriters, corkscrews, lamps and binoculars. The affable Serbian owner can give you a guided tour around every piece in his collection. Shop one (also at Týnská 7) has a smaller but similar range of curios.
☎ 224 815 763 ✉ Týnská 7, Staré Město
☯ 10am-7pm Ⓜ Náměstí Republiky

Dorotheum (7, E3) Venerable, upmarket gallery and auction house near the Estates Theatre, founded in 1707, and specialising in exquisite 19th- and early 20th-century glassware, porcelain and fine art, as well as some top-end furniture. Auctions are held at infrequent intervals; check the website for details.
☎ 224 222 001
🖳 www.dorotheum.cz
✉ Ovocný trh 2, Staré Město ☯ 10am-7pm

Mon-Fri, 10am-5pm Sat
Ⓜ Náměstí Republiky

Eduard Čapek (4, E2) The Čapek clan have lovingly operated their bric-a-brac shop since 1911 and nothing has ever been thrown away, including the dust. Rolls of recycled electric wire, rusty tools, dog-eared magazines and battered handbags are among the...er...treasures awaiting your perusal.
✉ Dlouhá 32, Josefov
☯ 10am-6pm Mon-Fri
Ⓜ Náměstí Republiky

Icons Gallery (2, B2) In the same building as Antique Music Instruments (see earlier), this cluttered little shop has a luminous selection of Russian and East European icons, as well as numerous other decorative *objets d'art*, watches, porcelain and Art Nouveau glassware.
☎ 233 353 777
✉ Pohořelec 9, Hradčany
☯ 9am-6pm Ⓜ Malostranská, then tram 22 or 23 to Pohořelec

Spend hours shopping or dreaming amongst the gorgeous wares at Art Deco Galerie

MUSIC

AghaRTA Jazz Centrum
(4, F6) Inside the esteemed AghaRTA club is a selection of the best Czech and world jazz CDs for the purist to ponder over. Pick up some Miles Davis and Chet Baker, or if you're in an experimental mood, try some of the latest from Prague performers like Jiří Stivín and Luboš Andršt.
☎ 222 211 275
✉ Krakovská 5, Nové Město 🕑 5pm-midnight Mon-Fri, 7pm-midnight Sat-Sun Ⓜ Muzeum

Andante Music (5, C3) This small shop specialising in classical music CDs has most of the big names covered, with a comprehensive collection of Czech and foreign composers. It also sells tickets to classical concerts in town.
☎ 257 533 718
✉ Mostecká 26, Malá Strana 🕑 10am-6pm Ⓜ Malostranská

Bazar (4, F6) There's a vast selection of second-hand CDs, LPs and videos to browse through here, representing a wide array of genres. Czech and Western pop jostle with jazz, blues, heavy metal, country and world music, though with CDs costing from roughly 300-400Kč, it's not exactly bargain basement.
☎ 602 313 730
🖥 www.cdkrakovska.cz
✉ Krakovská 4, Nové Město 🕑 9am-7pm Mon-Fri, 10am-2pm Sat Ⓜ Muzeum

You'll find what you're looking for at Philharmonia

Bontonland (4, E4) Purportedly the biggest music 'megastore' in the Czech Republic, this place covers pretty much everything, including Western chart music, classical, jazz, dance and heavy metal, as well as an extensive collection of Czech pop. It also sells videos and DVDs, and has a large Playstation arena and Internet access (1.50Kč per hour).
☎ 224 473 080
🖥 www.bontonland.cz
✉ Václavské náměstí 1, Nové Město 🕑 9am-8pm Mon-Sat, 10am-7pm Sun Ⓜ Můstek

Maximum Underground (7, C3) In an arcade off Jilská, this place is stocked with CDs and LPs of indie, punk, hip-hop, techno and other contemporary genres. It also has a selection of new and second-hand street- and club-ware for those after a Central European grunge look.
☎ 222 541 333 ✉ L1, Jilská 22, Staré Město 🕑 11am-7pm

Velvet Underground Revolution

What do a Czech political campaign and the sounds emitted by Reed, Cale and Co have in common? Well, Velvet Underground's music reportedly made inspirational listening for Václav Havel and fellow dissidents during communist rule. Havel finally met his idol when he interviewed Reed for *Rolling Stone* in 1990 and a bond was established between the one-time anti-establishment figures, leading to subsequent get-togethers. Havel also hit it off with his other musical heroes, the Rolling Stones, who have made a number of trips to the Czech capital; during their 2003 tour, Mick Jagger even chose to celebrate his 60th birthday in Prague.

Mon-Sat, noon-7pm
Sun Ⓜ Můstek,
Staroměstská

Music Antiquariat (4, D5) Take your time and browse through some of the thousands of new and second-hand rock 'n' roll, pop, jazz, classical and blues LPs and CDs in this well-stocked music store. The shop is dominated by its extensive vinyl collection, where you can find everything from Max Bygraves to Metallica, with a heavy dose of Neil Diamond along the way.
☎ 221 085 268 ✉ L1 Palác Metro, Národní 25, Nové Město ☾ 10.30am-7pm Mon-Sat Ⓜ Národní Třída

Philharmonia (7, C1) Sample the classics at this superbly stocked store, where you'll find the work of top Czech composers Dvořák, Janáček and Smetana. You'll also find jazz, Czech folk music, Jewish music and an eclectic selection of 'marginal genres', including rockerbilly, blues and other random offerings.
☎ 224 811 258 ✉ Pařížská 13, Josefov ☾ 10am-6pm Ⓜ Staroměstská

Trio Music Shop (7, C2) Trio is devoted to classical, Czech jazz and regional folk recordings. Pick up your favourite Beethoven or Brahms CD, or get folky and delve into Moravian outlaw songs or Wallachian drinking tunes.
☎ 222 322 583 ✉ Náměstí Franze Kafky 3, Staré Město ☾ 10am-7pm Mon-Fri, 10am-6pm Sat-Sun Ⓜ Staroměstská

Týnská Galerie (7, D2) This place stocks a good selection of classical CDs if you're after a little night music with Mozart or want to experience Dvořák's *New World*. It's also a ticket outlet for many classical concerts and recitals around Prague.
☎ 224 826 909 🖳 www.viamusica.cz ✉ Staroměstské náměstí 14, Staré Město ☾ 10am-8pm Ⓜ Staroměstská

BOOKS

Academia Bookshop (4, F5) Czech-language academic and scientific tomes dominate the upper floors of this big bookshop, while downstairs you can leaf through English novels, travel guides, maps and assorted titles on Prague.

Kanzelsberger for books

☎ 224 223 511 ✉ Václavské náměstí 34, Nové Město ☾ 9am-8pm Mon-Fri, 9.30am-7pm Sat, 9.30am-6pm Sun Ⓜ Můstek

Anagram (7, E2) Excellent English-language bookshop, with a vast range of novels and nonfiction, covering subjects such as European history, philosophy, religion, art and travel. There are also Czech works in translation and children's books. Seek out the remainders section for some bagain new and second-hand offerings on various topics.
☎ 224 895 737 🖳 www.anagram.cz ✉ Týn Court 4, Staré Město ☾ 10am-8pm

Mon-Sat, 10am-6pm Sun Ⓜ Náměstí Republiky

Antikvariát (7, D2) Antiquarian bookshop with a sizeable stock of mostly Czech and German titles, on a variety of topics. It also stocks an interesting collection of old prints, aquatints and maps to browse through.
☎ 224 895 775 ✉ Týn Court 2, Staré Město ☾ 10am-7pm Ⓜ Náměstí Republiky

Big Ben (7, E1) Well-stocked English-language bookshop, with shelves devoted to Prague reference books, travel, children's literature, science fiction, poetry and the

latest bestsellers. Various magazines and newspapers are also at hand.
☎ 224 826 565 ✉ Malá Štupartská 5, Staré Město ⏱ 9am-6.30pm Mon-Fri, 10am-5pm Sat-Sun Ⓜ Náměstí Republiky

Fraktaly (4, D4) This overflowing bookshop boasts an assortment of titles in English and Czech on architecture, design, art, photography and associated topics. They also stock English-language periodicals such as *Wallpaper*, and other arty magazines.
☎ 222 222 186 ✉ Betlémské náměstí 5a, Staré Město ⏱ 10am-9pm Ⓜ Národní Třída

Globe (4, C6) Popular hang-out for book-hunting backpackers, with a quiet cafe in which to peruse your purchases. There's lots of new fiction and nonfiction and English magazines, plus a big selection of second-hand novels.
☎ 224 934 203 ✉ Pštrossova 6, Nové Město ⏱ 10am-midnight Ⓜ Karlovo Náměstí

Kanzelsberger (4, E5) This huge bookstore has a good selection of translations of Czech authors, including Václav Havel's works, and various English-language novels. Books in French, German, Spanish and Italian are also available.
☎ 224 219 214 💻 www.dumknihy.cz/ram.htm ✉ Václavské

Try Anagram Bookshop, for English-language books

náměstí 4, Nové Město ⏱ 9am-8pm Ⓜ Můstek

Palác Knih Neo Luxor (4, F5) Giant bookshop selling miscellaneous books in English, German and other languages, including Czech authors in translation and travel guides. There's also a good selection of maps, international magazines and newspapers, as well as Internet access (1Kč per hour).
☎ 221 111 336 💻 www .dumucebnicaknih.cz ✉ Václavské náměstí 41, Nové Město ⏱ 8am-8pm Ⓜ Muzeum

Prospero (7, E2) In a passageway backstage of Celetná ulice is this theatre literature specialist. Knowledgable staff can guide you to new and second-hand tomes on dramatic happenings in the Czech Republic, plus thespian videos and CDs.
☎ 224 809 156 ✉ Celetná 17, Staré Město ⏱ 11am-5.30pm Mon-Fri Ⓜ Náměstí Republiky

A Multi-Story City

Prague has fuelled the imagination of many Czech authors and literary visitors. The ghost of Franz Kafka undoubtedly haunts the most claustrophobic of city laneways, in keeping with the smothering, obstacle-laden spirit of *The Castle* and *The Trial*. Gustav Meyrink put a suitably dark spin on the city's favourite legend in *The Golem*, while another Czech who prefers the less-lit path is Milan Kundera, who set *The Unbearable Lightness of Being* here.

Bruce Chatwin made Josefov the landscape of his novella about a porcelain collector, *Utz*. And former Czech president Václav Havel began his writing career as resident playwright of the Theatre on the Balustrade — check out his inspirational collection of early 1990s speeches and writings, *The Art of the Impossible*.

FOOD & DRINK

Albio (4, G2) Organic, wholefood and 'green' products fill this mini-market, where, amongst other things, you can pick up fruit and veg, tea, wine, fresh bread and soy products. Also stocks natural laundry detergents, cosmetics and the like. There's a wholefood restaurant next door (p68). ☎ 222 317 902 🖳 www.albiostyl.cz ✉ Truhlářská 20, Nové Město 🕑 7.30am-7.30pm Mon-Fri, 8am-2pm Sat Ⓜ Náměstí Republiky

Cellarius (4, F5) On sale are over 1500 fine wines from across the globe. France, Italy and Spain are well represented, while there are smaller selections of vino from South Africa, Australia and other New World producers. ☎ 224 210 979 🖳 www.cellarius.cz ✉ Lucerna Passage, Štěpánská 61, Nové Město 🕑 9.30am-9pm Mon-Sat, 3-8pm Sun Ⓜ Muzeum

Country Life (7, C3) This bulk health-food offshoot of

Markets in the Air

Prague has a few open-air markets to scatter money in, most of them open daily (some closed Sunday) from early morning to dusk. The most prominent (and priciest) is the food and trinket emporium on **Havelská** (7, C4; see pic below), which started life as a collective of specialist markets for German merchants around 1230.

Less-distinguished but less-costly markets, where cheap clothes elbow mounds of perfume, alcohol and toys, include the stalls at **Florenc** (4, J2), the vendors near Hradčanská metro (6, B3) at **Dejvice**, and the commercial sprawl at **Bubenské nábřeží** (6).

Every day is market day at Havelská Market

the popular vegie restaurant experiences lots of through-traffic due to its deliciously healthy organic juices, grains and other produce. Could easily claim Prague's biggest range of soy salamis.

☎ 224 213 366 ✉ Melantrichova 15, Staré Město 🕑 8.30am-7pm Mon-Thu, 8.30am-6pm Fri, 11am-6pm Sun Ⓜ Můstek

Fruits de France (4, F5) Gallic gastronomes and Francophile foodies will make a beeline for this consumables shop and its stash of fine wines, cheeses, vegetables and all manner of fresh, canned and bottled French fare. ☎ 224 220 304 ✉ Jindřišská 9, Nové Město 🕑 9.30am-6.30pm Mon-Fri, 9.30am-1pm Sat Ⓜ Můstek

Inside Country Life for those who like healthy eating

Havelská Market (7, C4) To the untrained eye, long-established Havelská Market can look like the archetypal tourist-trap bazaar, where shoppers snap up gaudy marionettes, souvenir tankards, tacky T-shirts and the like. But the self-sufficient should check out the fresh fruit and veg, and tasty treats like homemade gingerbread.
✉ Havelská, Staré Město
🕐 8am-6pm Ⓜ Můstek

Stay outside Country Life if you're only into junk food

La Casa de Cigarros y del Vino (7, E4) Hidden away inside the Černá Růže shopping centre, this aromatic shop sells quality international wines, both from the usual suspects such as France, Spain and California, and from more unusual sources, including Israel, Romania and, naturally enough, the Czech Republic. Cigars are also abundant.
☎ 221 014 716 ✉ Na příkopě 12, Nové Město

🕐 9am-8pm Mon-Fri, 9am-7pm Sat, 11am-7pm Sun Ⓜ Můstek

Pivní Galerie (6, D2) Some think Czech beer begins and ends with Pilsener Urquell, but a visit to the tasting room at Pivní Galerie should set them right. Here you can sample and buy a huge range of Bohemian and Moravian beers from the country's 30-plus microbreweries.
☎ 220 870 6 13 ✉ U Průhonu 9, Holešovice
🕐 10am-8pm Mon-

Fri, 10am-3pm Sat
Ⓜ Nádraží Holešovice

Sapori Italiani (4, D5) Those longing for a taste of Bella Italia should find satisfaction in this delicatessen, with its fine stock of Italian wines, cheeses and meats. Pasta and pasta sauces are also available, along with other tinned and bottled goods.
☎ 224 234 952
✉ Perlová 10, Nové Město 🕐 10am-7pm Mon-Fri, 11am-5pm Sat-Sun Ⓜ Můstek

FOR CHILDREN

Art Dekor (7, E3) This charmingly old-fashioned store overflows with handmade stuffed animals in a variety of colourful fabrics sure to delight any toddler. So, whether it's a green teddy, a cat covered in blue sailing boats or a batik elephant you have in mind, call in here.
☎ 221 637 178
✉ Ovocný trh 12, Nové Město 🕐 10am-7pm Mon-Sat, 10am-6pm Sun
Ⓜ Můstek

Dětský Dům (7, E4) Bright modern mall devoted to kids' stuff, with a number of separate specialist outlets selling such things as model cars, video games and stuffed toys. Other shops here sell children's shoes and trendy clothes for the little ones who just have to have Kenzo.
☎ 272 142 401 ✉ Na příkopě 15, Nové Město
🕐 9.30am-8pm Mon-Sat, 10am-6pm Sun
Ⓜ Můstek

Smiling Dětský Dům

Mothercare (7, E3) If you're travelling with a baby or very young child, you'll find pretty much everything you need to meet their non-edible demands in this bright and modern baby shop. Toys, clothes, accessories and all manner of other goods for mother and child are at hand.
☎ 222 240 008
🖳 www.mothercare.cz
✉ Pasáž Myselbek, Nové Město 🕑 9am-7pm
Ⓜ Náměstí Republiky

Sparky's Toy Shop for big kids, and little ones too

Pohádka (7, E2) It's marionettes galore in this overbrimming toy store, with a vast range of puppets, from fairy-tale favourites to more modern figures such as Harry Potter and, curiously, Louis Armstrong. Upstairs there's an assortment of simple wooden toys and dolls. The proliferation of 'Don't Touch' signs seems rather optimistic however.
☎ 224 239 469
✉ Celetná 32, Staré Město 🕑 9am-8pm
Ⓜ Náměstí Republiky

Sparkys (7, E3) Inviting toy store, with lots of stuffed animals from small to extra huge, as well as model cars, computer games, board games and cartoon videos and DVDs. Another branch, in Slovanský Dům, sells baby clothes, prams and toys for tots.
☎ 224 239 309
🖳 www.sparkys.cz
✉ Havířská 2, Staré Město 🕑 10am-7pm Mon- Sat, 10am-6pm Sun
Ⓜ Můstek

SPECIALIST STORES

Botanicus (7, E1) Prepare for olfactory overload in this ever-busy outlet for natural health and beauty products. The scented soaps, such as banana and yoghurt and blackberry and apple always draw a crowd, and you can rummage through shelves laden with intriguing herbal bath oils, shampoos, fruit cordials, herbal teas and handmade paper products.
☎ 224 895 445
✉ Týn Court 3, Staré Město 🕑 10am-8pm
Ⓜ Náměstí Republiky

Vinegar looks as appealing as wine at Botanicus

Cat's Gallery (7, D2) If you like cats, you'll love Cat's Gallery, with its colourful collection of cat kitsch. Cat-emblazoned T-shirts, cups, calendars and clocks

Handmade soaps at Botanicus make great gifts

can all be had, or perhaps you're just looking for an anthropomorphic ceramic cat smoking a cigar? Look no further!

✉ **Týnská 9, Staré Město**
🕑 **10am-7pm**
Ⓜ **Náměstí Republiky**

Hudy Sport (4, G3) One of the half-dozen Hudy Sport shops around Prague providing reasonably priced equipment for hiking, climbing, camping and other outdoorsy activities. There's a good selection of boots, backpacks, sleeping bags, tents, waterproofs and the like, as well as more specialist equipment like crampons and climbing picks.

☎ **224 813 010**
💻 **www.hudy.cz**
✉ **Havlíčkova 11, Nové Město** 🕑 **9am-6.30pm Mon-Fri, 9am-1pm Sat**
Ⓜ **Náměstí Republiky**

Karel Vávra (3, A3) Handmade fiddles decorate the interior of this old-fashioned violin workshop, where Karel and his assistants beaver away making and repairing the instruments in a time-honoured fashion. Even if you're not in search of a custom-made violin, it's worth a look just for the time-warp atmosphere.

☎ **222 518 114**
✉ **Lublaňská 65, Vinohrady** 🕑 **9am-5pm**
Ⓜ **IP Pavlova**

Orientální Koberce Palacka (3, B1) Sumptuous showroom filled with handmade carpets, rugs and wall-hangings from Iran and other central Asian states. The colourful pieces come in all sizes, and prices, in intricate traditional designs, and the knowledgeable staff will be happy to help you make an informed purchase.

☎ **541 214 620**
✉ **Vinohradská 42, Vinohrady** 🕑 **10am-7pm Mon-Fri, 10am-2pm Sat**
Ⓜ **Náměstí Miru**

Sanu-Babu (7, C3) Sandalwood-scented hippie heaven selling all manner of far-out New Age essentials, including incense sticks and holders, bongs, handmade Nepalese paper, wooden carvings and a colourful range of Nepalese clothes.

☎ **221 632 401**
💻 **www.sanubabu.cz**
✉ **Michalská 20, Staré Město**
🕑 **10.30am-10.30pm**
Ⓜ **Můstek**

Herbal lotions at Botanicus, in eye-catching bottles

Eating

In recent years, Prague has played host to an international gastronomic renaissance, and you can now sample everything from Afghan to Japanese cuisine if the standard Czech fare of roast meats and dumplings begins to pall. Don't write off Czech cuisine, though, as there are plenty of restaurants and pubs serving top-quality, and often very cheap local food, or excellent gourmet establishments creatively adapting it with a fresh international approach in mind.

The average Czech day includes breakfast (*snídaně*) with bread (*chléb*), cheese, ham, eggs and coffee, eaten at home or at one of the many, simple *bufety* (self-service places). Lunch (the main meal of the day) or dinner (*oběd*) consists of soup (*polévka*) and often the ubiquitous dumplings (*knedlo*), sauerkraut (*zelo*) and roast pork (*vepřo*). Other favoured items, particularly in pubs, include pork sausages (*buřt*) and goulash (*guláš*). Pretzels are often found on pub tables – you'll be charged when you leave for what you take.

Less pleasurable is an extra-large serving of sour-faced waiter indifference. But this isn't always the natural state of affairs and you have the option of either trying to break through the facade with some Czech words or good humour, or (as most do) just ignoring it. It'll be harder

to ignore the cigarette smoke that clouds most establishments, except at lunchtime when the custom is to refrain until lunch is finished.

A place calling itself a *restaurace* should be a cheaper restaurant, but often isn't. A *vinárna* is a wine bar that will mainly serve bite-sized items. A *kavárna* is a cafe, which in Prague usually means alcohol prevails as much as coffee, and food is restricted to snacks. Restaurant hours vary markedly, as do kavárna times, with many in the centre staying open late most nights; pubs are usually open from 11am to 11pm.

HRADČANY

Café Poet (5, A2) $$
Cafe
Tourist cafe with an outdoor area set in a courtyard off the castle. Pricey, but a little less so than similar eateries. Re-energise yourself with sausages, pasta or salads, or just relax with a coffee.
☎ 224 373 599 ✉ Na Baště ⌚ 10am-6pm M Malostranská

Jídelní Lístek (2, A2) $
Modern Czech
Simple local hangout with a pleasant bar and an eclectic menu. Snacks such as fried mushrooms with cheese jostle with more substantial dishes like turkey curry, pork and cabbage, and fried carp.
☎ 220 516 731 ✉ Pohořelec 10 ⌚ 11am-8pm M Malostranská, then tram 22 or 23 to Pohořelec ♿ Ⓥ

Malý Buddha (2, B2) $
Vegetarian, Asian
Tea-and-vegetables temple transplanted from the Orient complete with a Buddhist shrine, and regularly crowded. Has 'healing wines' and teas to accompany the veggie meals. Also serves crab, shark and crocodile. Credit cards unpalatable.
☎ 220 513 894 ✉ Úvoz 46 ⌚ 1-10.30pm Tue-Sun M Malostranská, then tram 22 or 23 to Pohořelec ♿ Ⓥ

Oživlé Dřevo (2, A3) $$$$
Modern Czech
Wine and dine someone special in this rustic, cushion-strewn hall at the base of Strahov Monastery. Try the marinated venison, grilled turbot, or go for the 3-course fixed menus (from 990Kč). The garden terrace has superb views over Prague, though service can be achingly slow.
☎ 220 517 274 ✉ Strahovské nádvoří 1 ⌚ 11am-11pm M Malostranská, then tram 22 or 23 to Pohořelec

Peklo (2, A3) $$$-$$$$
Modern Czech
In the monastery compound, this subterranean cavern named 'Hell' in Czech, was once a medieval wine cellar. Today it's an eerily atmospheric venue for fine dining. The house speciality is trout, straight from the cellar pond, while old favourites like goulash and duck-and-dumplings make an appearance. Small kids' menu also available.
☎ 220 516 652 🖥 www.peklo.com ✉ Strahovské nádvoří 1 ⌚ 6pm-midnight Mon, noon-midnight Tue-Sun

M Malostranská, then tram 22 or 23 to Pohořelec ♿ Ⓥ

Sate (2, B2) $
Indonesian
Good-value restaurant, offering standards like *mie* & *nasi goreng*, *opor ayam* (chicken with coconut), Javanese beefsteak and a string of tasty vegetarian dishes.
☎ 220 514 552 ✉ Pohořelec 3 ⌚ 11am-10pm M Malostranská, then tram 22 or 23 to Pohořelec ♿ Ⓥ

U Labutí (2, C1) $$-$$$
Traditional Czech, Beer Hall
Once home to Tycho Brahe and Johannes Kepler, this grand medieval mansion today houses a popular restaurant and beer hall, with a converted stable, complete with troughs for messy eaters. Goulash, pork and dumplings and venison are among the menu items.
☎ 220 511 191 ✉ Hradčanské náměstí 11 ⌚ 10am-10pm M Malostranská ♿ Ⓥ

Great view, great place for a drink – Oživlé Dřevo

JOSEFOV

Ariana (4, E2) $$
Afghan
Friendly little place tucked down a side street with Afghan carpets, photos and knick-knacks for that semi-authentic feel. Try an Afghan curry or kebab or specialities such as *qabali uzbeki* (minced mutton with rice) while central Asian music wails in the background.
☎ 222 323 438 ✉ Rámová 6 🕑 11am-11pm Ⓜ Staroměstská

Chez Marcel (4, E2) $$
French & Breakfast
Sit back, sip a *pastis* while Edith Piaf warbles over the sound system and imagine you're on the Left Bank. Salads, omelettes and sandwiches feature, alongside substantial fare like rabbit in mustard sauce. There's also the latest French papers and magazines.
☎ 222 315 676
✉ Haštalská 12 🕑 8am-1am Mon-Fri, 9am-1am

Sat-Sun Ⓜ Náměstí Republiky 🚇 Ⓥ

Dahab (4, F2) $-$$
Middle Eastern
Cushion-covered benches and hookahs straight from the kasbah give this place an oriental ambience. The menu is almost wholly vegetarian, with couscous and salad dishes, as well as Arabian coffees and sweets. It's a shame the staff appear to be competing for the 'Worst Service In Prague' award.
☎ 224 827 375 ✉ Rybná 28 🕑 noon-1am
Ⓜ Náměstí Republiky Ⓥ

Dahab Yalla (4, F2) $
Middle Eastern
Inexpensive fast-food joint attached to the restaurant of the same name, with a good range of couscous, gyros, salads, soups and other light meals available.
☎ 224 827 375
✉ Dlouhá 33 🕑 10am-8pm Ⓜ Náměstí Republiky Ⓥ

Franz Kafka Café (7, B1) $
Cafe
Slurp *káva* surrounded by brooding shots of Prague in the wood-panelled front room, or flee into a dark rear alcove to ponder life's trials over a *pivo* or two. Also serves juices and teas, plus sandwiches and other snacks.
✉ Široká 12 🕑 10am-10pm Ⓜ Staroměstská

King Solomon (7, B1) $$$$
Kosher
Smart restaurant serving up traditional Jewish delicacies such as gefilte fish, carp and chicken soup, and some inventive recipes involving duck, venison and lamb. Vegetarians won't find much to munch though.
☎ 224 818 752
✉ Široká 8 🕑 noon-11pm Sun-Thu
Ⓜ Staroměstská 🚇

Kolkovna (4, D2) $$
Traditional Czech
A Pilsener Urquell pub in a triangular block of striking apartment buildings, with lots of beer-friendly dishes like pork pie and Czech regulars like goulash and roast duck with cabbage and dumplings.
☎ 224 819 701
💻 www.kolkovna.cz
✉ V Kolkovně 8
Ⓜ Staroměstská
🕑 11am-midnight

La Bodeguita del Medio (4, C3) $$$-$$$$
Cuban
International chain restaurant that's a spin-off from

Dealing With 'Bill'

'Bill' can be a fractious fellow in Prague restaurants. Often he ends up costing you more than you expect, and often you don't understand what he's trying to tell you. Here are some hints on coping with him.

Double-check your bill carefully as there are a few people working in Prague's eateries who either failed maths in school or got top marks in the 'overcharging' business elective. Stuff you'd take for granted back home often comes at a price in Prague — wave away items you didn't order or don't want. Finally, be aware that many places have a cover charge, and that tips can be included in your final amount.

Hemingway's favourite haunt in Havana. Upstairs there's a noisy bar, downstairs the restaurant serves up Cuban and Creole cuisine, including grilled prawns, fried octopus, lobster and roast duck. Live music, Cuban cigars and ceiling fans complete the scene.

☎ 224 813 922
🖳 www.bodeguita.cz
✉ Kaprova 5
🕒 10am-2am
Ⓜ Staroměstská

Lary Fary (4, E2) $$$
Fusion

There are a number of themed rooms in this restaurant, so you can choose to dine under a Buddha, in Moorish surrounds or amongst Moghul interior decor. The food is equally diverse, with offerings such as beef in Thai marinade and sweet & sour duck noodles.

☎ 222 320 154
🖳 www.laryfary.cz
✉ Dlouhá 30 🕒 11am-midnight Ⓜ Náměstí Republiky

Les Moules (4, D2) $$
Belgian, Café

This 'Belgian Beer Café' provides an authentic brasserie atmosphere for typical cuisine such as the eponymous mussels, *pommes frites*, and lots of fish dishes. The bar stocks a wide range of Belgian beers and good quality international wines.

☎ 222 315 022
🖳 www.lesmoules.cz
✉ Pařížská třída19
🕒 8am-midnight
Ⓜ Staroměstská

Marco Polo IV (4, C3) $$$-$$$$
Italian, Seafood

Top-end fish restaurant with a vaguely Venetian look. Charbroiled monkfish, grilled snapper and other denizens of the deep dominate the menu, though there are other choices, such as ginger duck sauté.

☎ 224 819 668
✉ Široká 4 🕒 noon-10pm Ⓜ Staroměstská

Nostress (4, D2) $$$-$$$$
Fusion

Ultra-fashionable 'fusion' restaurant planted with a small forest of bamboo and modern sculptures. Try the roast salmon with ginger and lime. There's a big selection of wines and some mouth-watering desserts, and a bar and separate gallery where you can pick up some oh-so-stylish furniture.

☎ 222 317 004
🖳 www.nostress.cz
✉ Dušní 10 🕒 8am-11pm Mon-Fri, 10am-11pm Sat-Sun Ⓜ Staroměstská

Orange Moon (4, E2) $$
Southeast Asian

The bright orange walls, paper lanterns and Asian photos provide the perfect ambience for the Thai, Burmese and Indian cuisines served here. Clear your sinuses with some of the spicier curry options (the menu gives you an accurate chilli index to select your own level of spice comfort).

☎ 222 325 119
🖳 www.orangemoon.cz
✉ Rámová 5
🕒 11.30am-11.30pm
Ⓜ Staroměstská Ⓥ

Outside Franz Kafka Café

Pravda (4, D2) $$$-$$$$
Fusion

For something special, choose a formal white cloth-covered table, and select from the international menu, which has dishes inspired by the cuisines of Italy, Thailand, Japan, New Zealand and South Africa, amongst others. Pan-fried sea bass, ostrich and lamb are some of the options.

☎ 222 326 203
✉ Pařížská 17 🕒 noon-1am Ⓜ Staroměstská

U Krkavců (4, F2) $$$-$$$$
Modern Czech

Tired of pork and dumplings? Then try this underground vault for something more exotic. Roebuck steak with pear, crocodile, kangaroo and ostrich are among the less conventional items on the menu. You could also luxuriate with a beluga caviar (1790Kč) starter.

☎ 224 817 264
✉ Dlouhá 25 🕒 noon-3pm & 6pm-midnight Apr-Oct, 6pm-midnight Nov-Mar Ⓜ Náměstí Republiky

MALÁ STRANA

Cantina (5, C2) $
Mexican
Convivial Latin eatery just opposite the Petřín Hill tramway, where you can dine under a ceiling of coffee-sacks on the usual array of chilli con carne, enchiladas, quesadillas and so on. There's also a well stocked cocktail bar.
☎ 257 317 173 ✉ Újezd 38 ⏱ noon-midnight Ⓜ Malostranská then tram 12, 22 or 57 to Újezd 🚶 Ⓥ

Černý Orel (5, C3) $$
Italian
The 'Black Eagle' is a smart Italian restaurant with a Czech twist, serving all the expected spaghetti, tagliatelle and bruscetta, plus the odd Czech intruder like goulash and a few grilled fish and roast meat dishes.
☎ 257 533 207 ✉ Malostranské náměstí 14 (entrance on Zámecká) ⏱ 11am-11pm Ⓜ Malostranská 🚶 Ⓥ

C'est La Vie (4, A5) $$$$
Modern Czech, French
Crisp white linen table-cloths, candles and Frank Sinatra crooning in the background…so don't ask for a hamburger. Instead, sit down to delectable dishes such as grilled trout in champagne sauce and beetroot carpaccio with seared beef and truffle oil. There's a riverside terrace if you prefer to dine alfresco.
☎ 257 321 511 ✉ Říční 1 ⏱ 11.30am-1am Ⓜ Národní třída then tram 6, 9 or 22 to Vítězná 🚶

David (5, B3) $$-$$$
Modern Czech
Hidden away on a side lane, this place specialises in game, with dishes such as guinea-fowl with ratatouille. There are also a few fishy options – try the marinated salmon with caviar. Abstract art by Prague painter Míchel Halva is on sale here too.
☎ 257 533 109 ✉ Tržiště 21

⏱ 11.30am-11pm Ⓜ Malostranská

Gitanes (5, C4) $$-$$$
Mediterranean
Gitanes looks as if the contents of an entire Mediterranean village have been swept up by a tornado and deposited inside its walls. Balkan delicacies like sauerkraut filled with mincemeat and rice, plenty of seafood and pasta, as well as wine from Croatia and Bosnia-Herzegovina are there to tickle your palette.
☎ 257 530 163 🖥 www.gitanes.cz ✉ Tržiště 7 ⏱ 11am-midnight Ⓜ Malostranská

Hergetova Cihelna (4, B3) $$$-$$$$
International
Trendy bar, restaurant and cocktail lounge with a great view of Charles Bridge from its riverside terrace. The menu sports such diverse dishes as yellow-fin tuna sashimi, porcine risotto and poached lemon sole, and take your pick from 150 cocktails on offer at, allegedly, Prague's longest bar.
☎ 257 535 534 🖥 www.cihelna.com ✉ Cihelná 2b ⏱ 10am-1am Ⓜ Malostranská Ⓥ

Kampa Park (4, A3) $$$$
Modern Czech, Seafood
Exclusive restaurant/bar complex claiming the northern end of Kampa, giving its clientele magical views of the river, particularly at night. Serves top-class international food and wine

---

Waiter, There's a View in My Soup

For great river views, try tucking into stuffed salmon at **Restaurant Nebozízek** (☎ 257 315 329; 5, B6; $$; Petřínské sady 411), or dine on the terrace of **Hergetova Cihelna**.

Hanavský pavilón (☎ 233 323 641; 4, B1; $$$; Letenské sady 173) is a neo-baroque 1891 pavilion with good seafood and views. **U Zlaté studně** (☎ 257 533 322; 5, C2; $$$; U Zlaté Studně 4), in the hotel of the same name, has a fantastic vista. Highest of them all is the **Tower Restaurant** (☎ 267 005 778; 6, D3; $$; Mahlerovy sady 1) in Žižkov's TV Tower.

to famous types who then get listed on the back of a brochure.

☎ 257 532 685 ✉ Na Kampě 8b ⏱ 11.30am-late Ⓜ Malostranská Ⓥ

Square (5, C3) $$$-$$$$
Mediterranean
Square has been going, in various forms, since 1874. Today, this chic restaurant specialises in tapas, pasta and seafood, serving such dishes as clam risotto and duck prosciutto with melon and quince. English breakfasts, omelettes and the like are served until 11.30am.

☎ 257 532 109 🖳 www .squarerestaurant.cz ✉ Malostanské náměstí 5 ⏱ 9am-1am Sun-Wed, 9am-3am Thu-Sat Ⓜ Malostranská

U Bílé Kuželky (4, A3) $-$$
Traditional Czech
This restaurant tries to accommodate a cafe, restaurant and jazz & blues club, confusing tourists who stumble into it off Charles Bridge. The mainstream Czech cuisine includes good *svíčková* (creamy vegetable sauce with sliced meat and dumplings). Entry is off Dražického náměstí.

☎ 257 535 768 ✉ Míšeňská 12 ⏱ 11am-11pm Ⓜ Malostranská

U Malířů (5, C4) $$$$
French, Seafood
Splendid, romantic Art Nouveau setting in a mid-16th-century building, where you can indulge in exemplary seafood such as flounder rolls stuffed with salmon and lobster in chardonnay

sauce. Bohemian dishes include venison and other game. Three-course set menus start at 1190Kč.

☎ 257 530 000 🖳 www.umaliru.cz ✉ Maltézské náměstí 11 ⏱ 11.30am-midnight Ⓜ Malostranská

U Maltézských rytířů (5, C4) $-$$$
Traditional Czech
Cosy olde-worlde restaurant with an extensive wine menu and an excellent value 'lunch special' (100Kč). Regular meals include such things as saddle of boar in briar sauce and grilled pike.

☎ 257 530 075 🖳 www.umaltezskychr ytiru.cz ✉ Prokopská 10 ⏱ 11am-11pm Ⓜ Malostranská ♿

U Tří Zlatých Hvězd (5, C3) $-$$
Traditional Czech
Touristy but still good-value

restaurant with attentive staff. The mystical murals make the place look like an alchemist's antechamber, and the usual Bohemian specialities are on offer, including onion soup, pork and dumplings and roast meats. The set menus (from around 180Kč) are very good value.

☎ 257 531 636 ✉ Malostranské náměstí 8 ⏱ 11.30am-11.30pm Ⓜ Malostranská

U Zavěšeného Kafe (5, A3) $
Cafe
Also known as the Hanging Coffee (ask about it), this place has featured heavily in the city's artistic past and has many loyal, intelligence-brewing followers, as symbolised by the sculpture of a figure with a coffee cup for a head.

✉ Úvoz 6 ⏱ 11am- midnight Ⓜ Malostranská

Cafe Culture to a Tea...
Since the mid-1990s, a number of smokeless, tranquil tearooms (čajovny) have won popularity in Prague.
U Božího Mlýna (☎ 222 519 128; 3, A3; Lublaňská 50) is a subterranean chill-out spot with a big list of teas and health drinks. **Pod stromen čajovým** (☎ 222 251 045; 3, C1; $; Mánesova 55) serves 130 kinds of tea, as well as Czech mead.
U zeleného čaje (☎ 257 530 027; 5, B3; $; Nerudova 19) offers such tea-based concoctions as 'boiling communist', 'grandmother's caress' and 'soaking dog'. **Modrá čajovna** (☎ 602 176 355; 5, B3; $; Jánský vršek 8) is in a peaceful Malá Strana side-street courtyard, while **Růžová čajovna** (☎ 222 245 894; 4, G5; $; Růžová 8) has a more modern whitewashed interior, plus live music, and lots of tea and tea-ware on sale upstairs.

NOVÉ MĚSTO

Albio (4, G2) $
Vegetarian, Health
This fresh-looking, friendly wholefood restaurant, decked out in lots of pine and ropes, sources all its food from local organic farmers, and has its own onsite bakery, library and information centre. Dishes include rye gnocchi with cabbage, whole-wheat pasta, and vegetarian salads.
☎ 222 317 902 ⌨ www .albiostyl.cz ✉ Truhlářská 18 ⏱ 11.30am-10pm Mon-Fri Ⓜ Náměstí Republiky ♿ Ⓥ

Café Screen (4, G2) $
Cafe
Futuristic looking cafe (Jetsons style), with its primary colours, translucent plastic seating and TV screens continually playing MTV. Pizzas, baguettes, salads and delicious stuffed savoury pancakes compose the menu, along with a list of gourmet coffees.
☎ 224 816 607 ✉ Na Poříčí 15 ⏱ 9am-midnight Ⓜ Náměstí Republkiy Ⓥ

Cafe Slavia (4, C5) $-$$
Cafe
Once famous literary cafe where artists, performers and patrons of the National Theatre would gather to sip coffee and chat. It's still a smart place with great views over the river, though these days it's more of a tourist hangout. Roast duck, goulash and pasta dishes are on the inexpensive menu.
☎ 224 239 604 ✉ Národní 1 ⏱ 8am-11pm Ⓜ Národní Třída ♿

Café Tramvaj (4, F5) $
Cafe
All aboard for lunch! Sandwiches, salads and pizzas are served up in this pair of vintage tramcars parked in the middle of Wenceslas Square, and while the food might be unexceptional, the novelty value will entrance younger kids.
☎ 724 072 753 ✉ Václavské náměstí 32 ⏱ 9am-midnight Mon-Sat, 10am-midnight Sun Ⓜ Můstek ♿ Ⓥ

Casa Mia (4, E6) $$$
Italian
One part pizzeria, one part lavishly decorated restaurant where fresh John Dory, sea bass and toadfish is expertly prepared and cooked at your table Mediterranean-style. The large courtyard terrace makes for a pleasant alfresco dining experience.
☎ 296 238 203 ✉ Vodičkova 17 ⏱ 11am-11pm Ⓜ Národní Třída

Dynamo (4, C6) $$
Modern Czech
Sleek eatery with good food and all the ultra-modern trimmings — wooden floor, lots of space between tables, arty pictures and lime-green walls. The

Get low and comfortable at futuristic Café Screen

menu is a mix of central European and Mediterranean, which means the combinations of foodstuffs are unpredictable.

☎ 224 932 020
✉ Pštrossova 29
🕐 11.30am-midnight
Ⓜ Národní Třída

East-West (4, F5) $
Fusion
Billed as a 'Native' restaurant, this little place serves some unusual options such as Tibetan chicken curry and trout with wild rice, as well as simple baked potato dishes. African masks, and, in surreal Czech fashion, photos of penguins, adorn the walls.

☎ 296 236 513
✉ Štepánská 61
🕐 noon-midnight
Ⓜ Muzeum Ⓥ

Green Tomato (4, G4) $
Pizzeria
This place has gone for the Art Nouveau salon effect, with lots of mirrors, fancy lampshades and gilt-framed paintings, which makes a pleasant, if slightly incongruous, setting for an inexpensive pizza parlour. There's an extensive menu of pasta dishes as well, and a bar.

☎ 224 232 271
✉ Jindřišská 18
🕐 10am-11pm Mon-Sat, noon-10pm Sun
Ⓜ Náměstí Republiky
♿ Ⓥ

Highland Restaurant (6, B4) $$
Steakhouse
Carnivores, Caledonian or otherwise, will enjoy

Corporate Cuisine

There are plenty of perfect places for deal-making, procrastinating, or plain entertaining. **Restaurant Flambée** (☎ 224 248 512; 7, B4; $$$$; Husova 5) is an exclusive cellar retreat, patronised by diplomats and Hollywood stars. Inside the Hilton Hotel is **Café Bistro** (☎ 224 842 727; 4, J1; $$$; Pobřežní 1), a good 24-hour place to casually impress a business connection. **La Perle de Prague** (6, B4; $$$$; see p70) is the ultimate in fashionable Prague chic, and **Oživlé Dřevo** (2, A3; $$$; see p63) has a great terrace and an upmarket Czech menu.

---

this place, serving up hefty portions of Scottish highland steaks in various forms. You can even delve into 'Sean Connery's Pocket' (steak filled with scrambled eggs, bacon and onion). It also has ostrich, kangaroo and pasta.

☎ 224 922 511
✉ Gorazdova 22
🕐 10am-11.30pm Mon-Fri, noon-11.30pm Sat-Sun
Ⓜ Karlovo Náměstí

Káva Káva Káva (4, E5) $
Cafe
Fine-coffee emporium in a snug corner of a courtyard off Národní. It has won the 'best coffee in Prague' title

three times, so it must be doing something right. Businesspeople, weary shoppers, tourists and locals alike frequent the place for a quick coffee and a muffin.

☎ 224 228 862
✉ Národní 37 🕐 7am-9pm Mon-Fri, 9am-9pm Sat-Sun
Ⓜ Můstek

Kavárna Imperial (4, G2) $
Café
Splendid Belle Époque coffee-house, lavishly decorated with yellow and cream ceramic tiling and mosaics throughout. The food, however, is a bit of an anticlimax, with unremarkable omelettes, curries and

Maybe you'll meet your favourite author at Cafe Slavia

salads on the menu. Stick to the coffees and cakes, and watch out for the stale doughnuts.

☎ 222 316 012 ✉ Na Poříčí 15 🕑 9am-11pm Ⓜ Náměstí Republiky 🛗 Ⓥ

La Perle de Prague (6, B4) $$$$
Seafood, French
Atop the Dancing Building, this formal restaurant has sweeping views and some of the best seafood in the city. Scallops in saffron sauce, poached turbot and lobster are there to drool over. There are also some excellent wines and top-notch desserts.

☎ 221 984 160 ✉ 7th flr, Dancing Building, Rašínovo nábřeží 80 🕑 7-10.30pm Mon, noon-2pm & 7-10.30pm Tue-Sat Ⓜ Karlovo Náměstí

La Ventola (4, F2) $
Pizzeria
Modern pizza place and bar with an unusual, though effective, transport-related interior-decor theme going on, and a largely local clientele. Good value pizzas go for about 115Kč.

☎ 224 818 892 ✉ Soukenická 7 🕑 9am-11pm Ⓜ Náměstí Republiky 🛗 Ⓥ

Lemon Leaf (6, C4) $-$$
Thai
The bright, spacious and plant-filled interior of this popular Thai place is immediately inviting. Traditional Thai curries and noodles share the menu with intriguing dishes such as grilled plaice marinated

Albio organic restaurant has its own bakery and library

in seaweed. There's also a cocktail bar and some outdoor seating.

☎ 224 919 056 🖥 www .lemon.cz ✉ Na Zderaze 14 🕑 11am-11pm Mon-Thu, 11am-12.30am Fri, 12.30pm-midnight Sat, 12.30pm-11pm Sun Ⓜ Karlovo Náměstí Ⓥ

Le Patio (4, D5) $$-$$$
Breakfast & Brunch
Overdecorated cafe fronting a lifestyle store, adorned with a multiplicity of odd light fittings and large nautical mementos. Society types meet here chit chat over baguettes and extended Continental breakfasts.

☎ 224 934 375 ✉ Národní třída 22 🕑 8am-11pm Mon-Fri, 10am-11pm Sat-Sun Ⓜ Národní třída 🛗

Novoměstský pivovar (4, E6) $-$$
Beer Hall
Brewery-restaurant complex that makes great beer (Novoměstský ležák) purely for the purpose of quenching the thirsts of patrons in its busy food areas. House specialities include creamy

beef sirloin with dumplings, and roasted pork-knee.

☎ 222 232 448 ✉ Vodičkova 20 🕑 10am-11.30pm Mon-Fri, 11.30am-11.30pm Sat, noon-10pm Sun Ⓜ Národní třída

Picante (4, F2) $
Mexican, Takeaway Café
Busy takeaway serving a vast range of nachos, burritos, tacos and other hot Mexican fast food at very reasonable prices. There are also plenty of vegetarian options.

☎ 222 322 022 ✉ Revoluční 4 🕑 24hrs Ⓜ Náměstí Republiky

Řecká Taverna (4, F2) $
Greek
As Greek as it gets in Prague, with blue and white interior and 1970's wall-size pics of crumbling Greek monuments. Calamari, souvlaki, moussaka and feta salad are prominent on the menu, though you can also play safe with fish and chips.

☎ 222 317 762 ✉ Revoluční 16 🕑 11am- midnight Ⓜ Náměstí Republiky

Restaurace MD Rettigové (4, F2) $$
Traditional Czech
This interesting place boldly claims to be the only restaurant in Bohemia named after Magdaleny Dobromily Rettigové, a Czech woman who penned a famous cookbook over 200 years ago. The menu comprises lots of pork and beef, aided by local favourite, the dumpling.
☎ 222 314 483
✉ Truhlářská 4
🕓 11am-11pm
Ⓜ Náměstí Republiky

Rocky O'Reilly's (4, F6) $
Pub Grub
Ignore the raucous Irish pub at the rear of the building (see p82) and take a seat in the calmer, rustic farmhouse-kitchen-like restaurant for excellent value pub grub. Enormous, all-day 'Irish' breakfasts, fish and chips, chicken curry and filling meals are on the menu.
✉ Štěpánská 32
🖳 www.rockyoreillys.cz
🕓 10am-1am
Ⓜ Muzeum

Taj Mahal (4, G6) $$-$$$
Indian
Hidden behind the National Museum, this brightly decorated Indian restaurant serves all the usual things, chicken tikka masala, kormas and vindaloos with Western tastes in mind. Live music most evenings.
☎ 224 225 566
✉ Škretova 10
🕓 11.30am-11.30pm Mon-Fri, 1-11pm Sat-Sun
Ⓜ Muzeum Ⓥ

U Fleků (4, C6) $$
Beer Hall
The 'oldest beerhouse' in Prague is a crowded tourist trap, with a seating capacity of 1200 and tacky cabaret shows for heaving busloads of Japanese tourists. Roast-meat-and-dumplings dishes prevail, alongside the dark beer brewed onsite. Predictably perfunctory service.
☎ 224 934 019
✉ Křemencova 11
🕓 9am-11pm
Ⓜ Národní třída ♿

Zahrada v Opeře (4, G6) $$$
Modern Czech, Fusion
It's all wicker seating, exotic plants and bizarre light fittings in this designer restaurant. The top-end international cuisine is so artfully presented it seems a desecration to eat it. Seafood, salads and meaty dishes top the menu, along with excellent wines.
☎ 224 239 685
✉ Legerova 75
🕓 11.30am-1am
Ⓜ Muzeum

Žofín (4, B6) $ & $$$$
Modern Czech
This neo-Renaissance palace was built on an island in the Vltava in the 19th-century and restored in the 1990s as a stunning location for a gourmet restaurant. Dine on lobsters beneath the chandeliers, or the separate garden restaurant, with children's play area, provides cheap and filling fare.
☎ 224 919 139
✉ Slovanský ostrov
🕓 11am-midnight
Ⓜ Karlovo Náměstí
♿ Ⓥ

Zvonice (4, G4) $$$-$$$$
Traditional Czech
Fancy dining in a belfry? Occupying the 7th and 8th floors of the Jíndříšská Tower, this unique and atmospheric restaurant specialises in hearty meat dishes and game, with lots of good Czech wine to go with it.
☎ 224 220 009
✉ Jíndříšská věž, Senovážné náměstí
🕓 11.30am-midnight
Ⓜ Náměstí Republiky

Enjoy the coffee and lavish decor at Kavárna Imperial

STARÉ MĚSTO

Beas (7, D1) $
Vegetarian
Small vegetarian dhaba hidden away in a little courtyard off Týnská. There's a simple menu of the lentil and chickpea variety, with a salad or two thrown in.
☎ 777 165 478 ✉ Týnská 19 ⏱ 8.30am-8pm Mon-Fri, 10am-6pm Sat-Sun Ⓜ Náměstí Republiky ♿ Ⓥ

Bohemia Bagel (7, D1) $
Takeaway Café, Breakfast
This is one of the best deals in town with inexpensive filled bagels, sandwiches, salads and English and American-style breakfasts on offer, together with 'bottomless' coffees and soft drinks. There's Internet access (1.50Kč/hour), a kids' play area, phones and noticeboards with adverts for accommodation, language lessons and second-hand cars.
☎ 224 812 560 🖳 www .bohemiabagel.cz ✉ Masná 2 ⏱ 7am-midnight Mon-Fri,

Country Life's vegetarian buffet is very popular

8am-midnight Sat-Sun Ⓜ Náměstí Republiky ♿ Ⓥ

Byblos (7, E1) $$
Lebanese
Not easy to find (stuck just inside a shopping mall behind Kotva), this is the place to come if you want tasty Levantine delicacies. The lamb sausages with lemon are particularly good, other dishes include shish-kebabs, stuffed aubergine and a range of *mezze* (appetisers). Portions are rather small.
☎ 221 842 121 🖳 www .biblos.cz ✉ Rybná 14 ⏱ 8am-midnight

Mon-Fri, 11am-midnight Sat-Sun Ⓜ Náměstí Republiky Ⓥ

**Clementinum
(7, A2)** $$-$$$
Modern Czech, French
Trendy melange of beautifully presented Czech and international cuisine, with dishes like boar with juniper berry sauce, honey-roasted duck and beef carpaccio with mustard. However, portions tend be somewhat 'nouvelle cuisine', so don't be too hungry when you come here.
☎ 224 813 892 ✉ Platnéřská 9 ⏱ 11am-11pm Ⓜ Staroměstská Ⓥ

Country Life (7, C3) $
Vegetarian
Highly popular buffet-style vegetarian food hall connected to the health food shop of the same name, with a menu of hot meals and salads. The ultra-healthy unprocessed, unrefined, non-dairy food is charged according to weight. Strictly no smoking.
☎ 224 213 366 ✉ Melantrichova 15

Going Green

Vegetarian food in Prague ranges from pure, lovingly prepared dishes (Albio; p68) to trendy ethnic variations (Dahab; p64) to some pretty poor imitations. Dedicated vegetarian restaurants are quite rare in the inner city.

Be wary of places that appear in generic 'Vegetarian' listings in tourist leaflets – quite often they exaggerate to get the trade. Except in authentic vegetarian places, check the ingredients in the dishes, as it's not uncommon for your potential veggie meal to include fish, or in some cases a fistful of ham.

⏱ 9am-8.30pm Mon-Thu, 9am-6pm Fri, 11am-8.30pm Sun Ⓜ Můstek ♿ Ⓥ

Ebel Coffee House (7, D2) $
Cafe
Perfectly placed coffee house, offering numerous custom blends, cocktails, milkshakes and bagels. The 'continental breakfast' (a bagel or croissant, latte or tea, and juice or yoghurt) is good value at 160Kč.
☎ 224 895 788 ✉ Týn Court 2 ⏱ 9am-10pm Ⓜ Náměstí Republiky

Francouzská (7, F2) $$$$
French
The grand main restaurant of the even grander Municipal House is a haven for fine dining. Coq au Vin, bouillabaisse and swordfish are some of the gourmet offerings, or you could opt for the cheaper 3-course 'quick lunch' menu (490Kč), which changes regularly.
☎ 222 002 770 ✉ Municipal House, Náměstí Republiky 5 ⏱ noon-4pm & 6-11pm Mon-Sat, 11.30am-3pm & 6-11pm Sun Ⓜ Náměstí Republiky ♿

Jáchymka (7,C1) $
Traditional Czech/Beer Hall
A reasonable selection of Czech standards is on offer here, of the pork-and-dumplings variety, and several different beers to wash it all down in good old Prague fashion.
☎ 224 819 621 ✉ Jáchymova 4 ⏱ 10am-11pm Ⓜ Staroměstská ♿

Jalapeños (7, A1) $$
Tex-Mex
The mock-adobe 'n' thatch work interior makes you want to run for a poncho, but you'll soon appreciate the bright airiness of this place. It serves Mexican standards like tacos, fajitas and nachos, lots of steaks and puts together a mean margarita.
☎ 222 312 925 ✉ Valentinská 8 ⏱ 11am-midnight Ⓜ Staroměstská ♿

Kavárna obecní dům (7, F2) $-$$
Cafe
Chandelier-lit cafe in the Art Nouveau Municipal House. Salads and sandwiches are staples, or you could plump for the 3-course 'tourist menu' (250Kč). The groaning dessert trolley is continually wheeled around to tempt you further, while live jazz bands tootle away in the corner.
☎ 222 002 763 ✉ Náměstí Republiky 5 ⏱ 7.30am-11pm Ⓜ Náměstí Republiky ♿ Ⓥ

Klub Architektů (4, D4) $$-$$$
Modern Czech
Claustrophobics and nyctophobics might not enjoy this cramped, candle-lit cellar restaurant, and it does get a little stuffy, but the inventive modern cuisine is excellent, with fascinating dishes such as lamb with juniper berries, figs and 'old Czech style gingerbread spices'.
☎ 224 401 214 ✉ Betlémské náměstí 5A ⏱ 11.30am-midnight Ⓜ Národní třída

La Provence (7, E2) $$$
French
Provencale and traditional French cuisine is on offer in elegant, if slightly haughty, surrounds. Coq au Vin, cassoulet and bouillabaisse are some of the features of the menu, and you can accompany your selections with an excellent bottle of Bordeaux.
☎ 257 535 050 🖳 www.laprovence.cz ✉ Štupartská 9 ⏱ noon-midnight Ⓜ Náměstí Republiky

Kavárna obecní dům is in the stunning Municipal House

Le Saint-Jacques (7, E2) $$$
French
In true French style, this is a simply elegant, family-run restaurant where you can be serenaded by a piano and violin over a candle-lit dinner. Pork, beef, fish and game dishes figure on the menu, as well as plenty of good French wine.
☎ 222 322 685
✉ Jakubská 4
🕐 noon-3pm & 6pm-midnight Mon-Fri, 6pm-midnight Sat Ⓜ Náměstí Republiky

Millhouse Sushi (7, F3) $-$$
Japanese
Tired of shopping? Sit up to the conveyor belt and help yourself to nigiri, sushi, sashimi, tempura and other Japanese mouthfuls in this bright, modern place in the courtyard of the Slovanský Dům shopping mall. Colour-coded dishes cost between 60Kč and 180Kč.
☎ 221 451 771
✉ Slovanský Dům, Na Příkopě 22 🕐 11am-11pm Ⓜ Náměstí Republiky Ⓥ

Plzeňská (7, F2) $$
Traditional Czech
In the basement of the Municipal House, this Art Nouveau hall is all stained glass, chandeliers and polished wood. Meat-heavy specialities like pork and rice, lamb stroganoff and Prague ham and gherkins dominate, though the odd vegetarian choice slips through.
☎ 222 002 780
✉ Náměstí Republiky 5
🕐 11.30am-11pm
Ⓜ Náměstí Republiky
♿ Ⓥ

Rasoi (4, E2) $$$
Indian
Everything from the chef down to the cutlery comes straight from India, so this is about as authentic as you're going to get in Prague. Popular main dishes include tandoori salmon, chicken jalfrezi and vegetable biryani and there's an extensive menu of other meaty and veggie options. Does a good mango lassi.
☎ 222 328 400
🖳 www.rasoi.cz
✉ Dlouhá 13 🕐 noon-

Sushi at Millhouse Sushi

11.30pm Ⓜ Náměstí Republiky ♿ Ⓥ

Reykjavík (7, A3) $$$-$$$$
Seafood, Scandinavian
Owned by Iceland's honorary consul-general in Prague, this place serves top-notch Nordic nosh like salted herrings, eel and, perhaps more palatably, salmon and chips. The menu gives you insightful titbits, such as the fact that 60% of Icelanders believe in elves, while the walls are inexplicably plastered with violins and half a piano.
☎ 222 221 218 🖳 www .reykjavik.cz ✉ Karlova 20 🕐 11am- midnight Ⓜ Staroměstská

Rybí trh (7, E1) $$$-$$$$
Seafood
One of Prague's most accomplished seafood restaurants, 'Fish Market', lives up to its name by acquiring fresh catches daily (see the mound of ice inside) and preparing it how you like it. Specialities include sushi, and lobster

The menu's great at Klub Architektů cellar restaurant

plucked from the internal aquarium.

☎ 224 895 447 ✉ Týn Court 5 🕑 11am-midnight Ⓜ Náměstí Republiky

Sarah Bernhardt (7, F2) $$$$
French, Modern Czech

They don't come much grander than this, an Art Nouveau feast for the eyes and a French/Czech treat for the tastebuds. The full gamut of gourmet dining is on offer, from caviar to lobster, though more affordable is Sunday Brunch (noon-4pm) for 750/375Kč with drinks.

☎ 222 195 195 ✉ Hotel Paříž, U Obecního domu 1 🕑 noon-4pm & 6pm-midnight Ⓜ Náměstí Republiky

Siam-I-San (7, A1) $$$
Thai, Vegetarian

There's plenty of glass in this upmarket restaurant, alongside the obligatory Buddhas. Dishes include *nuer sa wan* (pan-fried marinated beef) and *kra prao koong* (stir-fried prawns with chilli and assorted vegetables). The unique crockery, cutlery and glasses can be bought in the adjoining Arzenal.

☎ 224 814 099 ✉ Valentinská 11 🕑 10am-midnight Ⓜ Staroměstská Ⓥ

Tequila Sunrise (7, E2) $
Mexican

Though solidly aimed at the passing tourist traffic (viz the sombreros and Spanish dolls), Tequila Sunrise still turns out reasonably authentic tacos, fajitas, burritos and the like. There's also a convivial little bar at the front.

☎ 224 819 383 ✉ Štupartská 6 🕑 11am-11pm Ⓜ Náměstí Republiky

Týnská Literary Cafe (7, D2) $
Cafe

Publisher-run cafe patronised by moody literary types who want to be seen being moody. There's a pleasant courtyard where you can rub your chin while reading Kierkegaard, or chat over coffee and cakes, and there are occasional public readings.

☎ 224 827 807 🖥 www.knihytynska.cz ✉ Týnská 6 🕑 9am-11pm Mon-Fri, 10am-11pm Sat-Sun Ⓜ Náměstí Republiky

U Budovce (7, D2) $
Cafe

Popular place just off Old Town Square, where you'll be surrounded by antique mirrors and sewing-machine treadles. An assortment of light meals such as soups, salads and sandwiches is on offer.

☎ 222 325 908 ✉ Týnská 7 🕑 9am-midnight Ⓜ Náměstí Republiky Ⓥ

U Rotta (7, C3) $$
Traditional Czech

Down in the Gothic cellars beneath the crystal shop of the same name, this mock-medieval place offers 'original folklore shows' every night and Bohemian specialities like baked pork and beef. Pickled haggis also features on the menu.

☎ 224 229 529 ✉ Malé náměstí 3 🕑 11am-midnight Ⓜ Staroměstská

V Zátiší (4, C4) $$$-$$$$
Modern Czech

Declared central Europe's best restaurant in 2002 by Egon Ronay, this gourmet place serves excellent, and reasonably priced Czech and international cuisine. Try asparagus with truffle and Tokay wine dressing, and grilled langoustines or roast rabbit. The 3-course lunch menu, including a drink (weekdays only), is great value at 595Kč.

☎ 222 221 155 ✉ Liliová 1 🕑 noon-3pm & 5.30-11pm Ⓜ Můstek

For gourmet food at realistic prices come to V Zátiší

VINOHRADY

Alexander Veliki (3, A3) $-$$
Greek
Friendly cellar taverna specialising in Macedonian minced meat dishes. Fishy alternatives include shrimp kebabs and grilled salmon, and there's also a few veggie options and Czech standards like pork steaks.
☎ 222 517 789
✉ Lublaňská 59
🕑 11am-11pm
Ⓜ Náměstí Míru Ⓥ

Bumerang (3, A3) $$
Australian
Basement restaurant and bar appealing to homesick antipodeans and those in search of something a little different; yes, it's roast (or sautéed) kangaroo time again. Other offerings include t-bone steaks and mixed grills, and there's a well-stocked bar.
☎ 222 518 572
✉ Londýnská 52
🕑 11am-midnight Mon-Fri, 5pm-midnight Sat-Sun Ⓜ Náměstí Míru

Kojak's (3, B1) $$
Tex-Mex
The connection with the lollipop-sucking sleuth is vague, though otherwise this is a regular, sombrero-hat-bedecked haven for tacos, nachos, chimichangas and quesadillas. Veggie options, steaks and seafood are also available, and there's a delivery service.
☎ 222 250 594 ✉ Anny Letenské 16 🕑 11.30am-midnight Ⓜ Náměstí Míru ♿ Ⓥ

Stuff to Savour

Try these places to pump up your sugar levels or to take a break from the taste of goulash and dumplings. **Cream & Dream** (☎ 224 211 035; 7, B3; Husova 12) has lots of exotically swirled, fruity Italian ice creams. **Paneria** (☎ 224 827 401; 4, F2; Dlouhá 50) has tarts, sandwiches, and filled croissants and baguettes.

Gourmand au Gourmand (☎ 222 329 060; 7, A1; Dlouhá 10) has luscious tarts, cakes and pastries, and some of the best ice cream around.

Just look at those pastries at Gourmand au Gourmand

Mehana Sofia (3, B3) $-$$
Bulgarian
Downstairs in the hotel of the same name (see p101), this is an authentic slice of the Balkans, down to the boar-skins on the wall. Traditional Bulgarian dishes like *kebapcheta* (grilled sausages) and *kyufte* (meatballs) are on the menu. If you're feeling reckless, you might like to try the buttered tripe...
☎ 603 298 865 ✉ Americká 28 🕑 noon-11pm Ⓜ Náměstí Míru ♿ Ⓥ

Osmička (3, A1) $-$$
Modern Czech, Italian
This is an underground eatery packed with lots of old mirrors, chandeliers and paintings, and a battered piano in the corner. It serves traditional Czech specialities with a modern 'fusion' twist, such as roast duck in calvados sauce, as well as pasta dishes, steaks and fish.
☎ 222 826 211 ✉ Balbínova 8 🕑 11am-11pm Ⓜ Náměstí Míru

Rudý Baron (3, C2) $$
Modern Czech
You're not likely to find too many Red Baron-themed restaurants around, so if you have an unusual hankering to dine out beneath bi-plane propellers and photos of WWI German

air-aces, then this place is for you. For carnivores, the meaty items on the menu includes roast piglet, roast duck in honey and barbecue chicken.

☎ 222 513 610
✉ **Korunní 23** 🕑 **11am-midnight Mon-Fri, noon-midnight Sat-Sun** Ⓜ **Náměsti Míru**

Tiger Tiger (3, B1) $$
Thai
It may look outwardly unremarkable, but inside,

this is one of the best places in the city for Thai cuisine. Tasty specialities include chicken coconut soup, *som tam* (spicy carrot salad) and *pad thai* (fried noodles, tofu, tamarind, onions and egg), plus lots of traditional curries; to save face, heat levels are indicated on the menu.

☎ 222 512 084
✉ **Anny Letenské 5**
🕑 **11.30am-11pm Mon-Fri, 5pm-11pm Sat-Sun**
Ⓜ **Náměsti Míru** Ⓥ

Cream & Dream – yum!

WORTH A TRIP

Adriatico (6, D4) $$-$$$
Italian
It might not look much, but this little hideaway serves some of the best Italian food in Prague. Homemade ravioli stuffed with pears, polenta with truffles and lots of flavoursome pasta dishes make the trip worthwhile.

☎ 271 726 506
✉ **Moskevská 58 (entry on Na Spojce)** 🕑 **11am-11pm Mon-Fri, 1-11pm Sat-Sun** Ⓜ **Náměstí Miru then tram 4, 21 or 23 to Moskevská**

Corso (6, C2) $-$$
Italian, Traditional Czech
Though Corso has more ceiling decorations and painted glass than many churches, its menu is all straightforward pasta dishes and traditional Czech cooking. It also serves more than twenty different Czech wines if you fancy a tipple.

☎ 220 806 541
✉ **Dukelských Hrdinů 48**
🕑 **9am-11pm** Ⓜ **V-ltavská**

Hong Kong (6, C2) $$
Chinese
A huge menu, big servings, separate smoking and non-smoking areas, and good Chinese food are reasons why you should drop in if you're in the Bubeneč/Holešovice area. Staff even have the compassion to turn the Canto-pop down to a bearable level.

☎ 233 376 209
✉ **Letenské náměstí 5**
🕑 **11am-11pm**
Ⓜ **Hradčanská, then tram 1, 8, 25 or 26 to Letenské náměstí**

Rezavá Kotva (6, B4) $
Cafe
Perched on the tip of Dětský ostrov, this place has some great views downriver. There's a small indoor bar

and a breezy, open decking area where you can tuck into sandwiches, salads, baked potatoes and bigger meals such as chicken tandoori and grilled trout.

☎ 777 550 005
✉ **Dětský ostrov, Smíchov** 🕑 **9am-2am Mon-Sat, noon-midnight Sun** Ⓜ **Anděl** 🚻 Ⓥ

U Vyšehradské Rotundy (6, C5) $-$$
Italian, Traditional Czech
Just inside the Vyšehrad castle compound, this quiet place has a pleasant garden where you can enjoy beer and sausages and gaze at Prague's oldest Roman-esque rotunda. There's a big list of pizzas, gnocchi and the like, plus steak dishes.

☎ 224 919 970 ✉ **K rotundě 3, Vyšehrad**
🕑 **11am-11pm**
Ⓜ **Vyšehrad** 🚻

Entertainment

The history of this striking old city can't help playing a part in the exuberant local entertainment scene, be it providing a grand auditorium like Smetana Hall or several dozen churches in which to stage familiar and newly discovered operas, drama and classical concerts, or the atmospheric stone cellar of a centuries-old building in which Czech musicians blaze away on guitars, saxophones and vocal cords. There are plenty of more contemporary venues too, with ultramodern clubs, suave bars and refreshingly down-to-earth pubs.

Live jazz at subterranean Club Železná

Although there are places with almost exclusively Czech patronage and a fair few that fall headlong into the tourist trap category, most central places attract a mixed bunch. On the downside, in recent years, some central bars have been besieged by the largely British and Irish 'stag-party' crowd in search of cheap beer – and lots of it – and you'll see banning notices up in some places. The vast majority of pubs, thankfully, remain convivial and trouble-free. As for entertainment, Staré Město is riddled with theatres, bars and live-music joints, with some of the flashier ones crowded around Pařížská and in the maze of streets behind Týn Church – many good jazz spots lie between Old Town Square and Národní. Clubs are strewn from Smíchov to Holešovice and everywhere in-between, including the busy Malostranské

Drinking beer with view of St Nicholas Church

náměstí. The industrial landscape of Žižkov is home to some arty cinemas, experimental performance venues, and gay clubs – the gay scene isn't concentrated in one district but rather spread around the inner city. The area south of the National Theatre to Myslíková is one of the freshest, hippest zones, with a lot of young clubs, bars and cafes.

There are many publications with details of what's on, where, and if it's worth the bother. The 'Night & Day' section of the weekly *Prague Post* covers basically everything. *Heart of Europe* is a free glossy monthly with details of galleries, theatres, clubs and music; *Prague Monthly Guide* is a much briefer source of listings. *Houser* is a free Czech-language booklet slanted to hip youth, while *Prague This Month* and *Welcome to Prague* are free monthly tourist booklets with information on theatre, music and sport. *Amigo* magazine thoroughly covers the gay scene.

Special Events

January *Febiofest* – 25-31 January; International Festival of Film, Television & Video prompts screenings of new international films across the Czech Republic

March *AghaRTA Prague Jazz Festival* – until December; top-drawer jazz artists and orchestras play at AghaRTA and elsewhere in the city

April *Musica Ecumenica* – 7-16 April; International Festival of Spiritual Music, in various ethereal venues around town

Burning of the Witches (Pálení čarodějnic) – 30 April; not literally, just the traditional burning of brooms to ward off evil, accompanied by lots of backyard end-of-winter bonfires

Musica Sacra Praga – Easter, August, October; the Festival of Sacred Music takes place in a number of churches and concert halls, presenting material by Brahms, Puccini and Dvořák among others

May *Majáles* – 1 May; student-celebrated spring festival with a parade from Jana Palacha to Old Town Square

Festival of Chamber Music – 3 May to 3 June; tribute to Czech composers and Mozart at Bertramka, site of a Mozart Museum in Smíchov

Prague Spring (Pražské jaro) – 12 May to 4 June; International Music Festival, the most prestigious classical music event in Prague held at various concert halls, churches and theatres

June *ET Jam* – rock and alternative music gig at Autokemp Džbán camp site in Vokovice

Dance Prague (Tanec Praha) – 9-28 June; International Festival of Modern Dance, with innovative performances at various venues

Ethnic Festival – 17 June to 23 September; folklore performed at the Municipal Library theatre by traditionally costumed Czech and Slovakian ensembles

August *Verdi Festival* – to September; nothing but Verdi operas at the Prague State Opera

September *Burčak* – sweet, cider-like liquid syphoned off at the initial stage of fermentation of new grape crops, and available for only a few weeks every year

Mozart Iuventus – 4-29 September; Mozart Festival at Bertramka featuring young artists playing his tunes, plus compositions written for the occasion

Prague Autumn – 11 September to 1 October; same concept as the more esteemed Prague Spring International Music Festival, but in autumn. Held at the Rudolfinum and State Opera

Svatováclavské slavnosti – 16-28 September; St Wenceslas Festival of spiritual art, encompassing music, painting and sculpture

October *International Jazz Festival* – 24-27 October; traditional jazz at popular haunts like Lucerna Music Bar and Reduta

November *Musica Iudaica* – Festival of Jewish Music, focusing on the composers of Terezín

December *Festival Bohuslava Martinů (Bohuslav Martinů Music Festival)* – 7-13 December; classical music festival dedicated to a famous Czech composer of the 20th century

BARS & PUBS

Alcohol Bar (7, C1) The staggering selection of booze at this aptly named drinker's shrine includes 250 types of whisky and scarce gins and rums. It's spacious, so you don't have to worry about tottering into fellow connoisseurs, and it has a well-stocked humidor. Gets going late.
☎ 224 811 744
✉ Dušní 6, Staré Město ☽ 7pm-2am
Ⓜ Staroměstská

Barfly (4, C4) Snug cellar spot with a laid-back ambience, perfect for those evening drinks with someone special. It has a particularly good selection of Czech wines and serves lots of pasta dishes and house specialities like steak tatar.
☎ 222 222 141
🖳 www.barfly.cz
✉ U Dobřenských 3, Staré Město ☽ noon-2am Mon-Sat, noon-midnight Sun
Ⓜ Národní Třída

Bloody Freddy Bar (4, D4) Trendy little bar hidden away on a side street off Michalská, popular with local youth and backpackers alike. There's a long menu of powerful cocktails on offer, including some curious absinthe concoctions, and a selection of salads and sandwiches to munch while watching whatever happens to be on the Eurosport channel.
✉ Vejvodova 6, Staré Město ☽ 4pm-2am
Ⓜ Můstek

Getting into Top Beer

Pivo means beer and it's one of the most frequently uttered (though not always intelligible) words in a republic whose citizens distinguish themselves by being the biggest consumers of beer in the world, downing on average 160L per person each year. The most popular of the many fine and inexpensive local brews are Pilsener Urquell and Gambrinus. Other brands include Staropramen and Budvar (the original and better Budweiser), plus the output of many excellent microbreweries.

The 10, 12 or other numeral designated to beers along with a degree symbol thankfully doesn't represent alcohol content. It's a measurement of the density of the pre-fermentation beer mixture – 10° beers are dark beers, while 12° are generally lighter.

Blue Light (5, C3) Suitably dingy and atmospheric jazz cavern, where you can enjoy a relaxed drink and cast an eye over the vintage posters and records that deck the walls. Unfortunately, the jazz itself comes in recorded rather than live form.
☎ 257 533 126
✉ Josefská 1, Malá Strana ☽ 6pm-3am
Ⓜ Malostranská

Bombay Cocktail Bar (4, E2) Upstairs from Rasoi (p74), this is an elegant,

laid-back place to sip a sidecar or a Tom Collins or two. The cocktail list goes on and on, and the nightly DJ is more than happy to take requests.
☎ 222 324 040
✉ Dlouhá 13, Staré Město ☽ 4pm-4am
Ⓜ Náměstí Republiky

Boulder Bar (4, E6) Sporty looking pub with an unusual take on interior decor, with oars and kayaks dangling from the ceiling. If it all makes you feel like climbing the walls, you can — there's an artificial climbing wall at the back for you to work up a thirst.

☎ 222 231 244

🖥 www.boulder.cz

✉ V Jámě 6, Nové Město

$ 60Kč for 2hrs, 70Kč after 5pm ⏲ 10am-midnight Mon-Fri, noon-midnight Sat-Sun; climbing wall 8am-10pm Mon-Fri, noon-10pm Sat, 10am-10pm Sun Ⓜ Muzeum

Chateau (7, E2)
Very red, British pub-like establishment, where the cheap beer never fails to attract a night-time crowd. Everything in this pointedly cool bar is backlit, including the smiles of the clientele; black T-shirt compulsory.

☎ 222 316 328

🖥 www.chateau-bar.cz

✉ Jakubská 2, Staré Město ⏲ noon-3am Mon-Thu, noon-4am Fri, 4pm-4am Sat, 4pm-2am Sun Ⓜ Náměstí Republiky

James Joyce (7, A4)
This often-raucous Irish pub serves Guinness and reasonably priced bar-meals to a mixed clientele of backpackers, expats and a scattering of locals. Regularly heaving, especially around lunchtime.

☎ 224 248 793

🖥 www.jamesjoyce.cz

✉ Liliová 10, Staré Město ⏲ 10.30am-12.30am Ⓜ Staroměstská

Jo's Bar (5, C3)
Longstanding backpacker haunt, upstairs from the Garáž club (p84), with an ever-crowded little bar/restaurant and satellite TV. Nachos, burritos and pasta dishes are served to accompany the beer.

☎ 257 451 271

✉ Malostranské náměstí 7, Malá Strana ⏲ 11am-late Ⓜ Malostranská

Konvikt Pub (4, D5)
Good, honest, old-time pub populated by refreshed locals and the odd tourist taking a well-earned gulp between classical concerts. Avoids the raucousness of similar places and serves tasty Czech meals.

☎ 224 232 427

✉ Bartolomějská 11, Staré Město ⏲ noon-1am Ⓜ Národní Třída

Legends Sports Bar (7, D2)
With 16 TV screens showing everything from British football to NFL action, this place can easily claim to be Prague's biggest and most popular sports bar. It isn't that big, however, and gets very crowded very quickly. Huge cocktails list, lots of burgers, all-day breakfasts and the like on offer.

☎ 224 895 404

🖥 www.legends.cz

✉ Týn Court 1, Staré Město ⏲ 11am-1am Sun-Wed, 11am-3am Thu-Sat Ⓜ Náměstí Republiky

Marquis de Sade (7, E2)
High-ceilinged den of liquidity, where absinthe is thrown back among decrepit red-velour couches, scruffy saloon tables, and sinfully large artwork. The building was a brothel in a previous life, hence the small 'viewing' balcony upstairs; nowadays it's the bar staff who look after the demanding clientele.

☎ 224 817 505

✉ Templová 8, Staré Město ⏲ 11am-2am Ⓜ Náměstí Republiky

Ocean Drive (4, E2)
There's a touch of American West Coast chic about this slightly precious cocktail bar

Choose your own poison at 'Cuban-Irish' pub, O'Che's

for local fashionistas and friends. It's a wonderfully stylish place, though, and a pleasant place to while away the evening over a gimlet. There's a predictably huge range of excellent cocktails.
☎ 224 819 089
✉ V kolkovně 7, Staré Město ☽ 7pm-2am
Ⓜ Staroměstská

O'Che's (7, A3) The only revolutionary spirits you'll find in this 'Cuban-Irish' pub are on the shelves behind the paraphernalia-riddled bar. Caters to sports-starved drinkers who need a dose of football or rugby with their Guinness, and dishes out reasonable blackboard specials to soak up your tipple.
☎ 222 221 178
🖥 www.oches.com
✉ Liliová 14, Staré Město ☽ 10am-1am
Ⓜ Staroměstská

Pivnice Na Ovocném trhu (7, E3) If the tiny, gloomy interior of this old-fashioned pub is not to your liking, there are plenty of seats out on the cobblestones, complete with festive parasols. It's a relaxing spot, watched over by the Estates Theatre, and there's a menu of the usual Czech dishes.
☎ 224 211 955
✉ Ovocný trh 17, Staré Město ☽ 11am-10pm
Ⓜ Náměstí Republiky

Pivovarský Dům (6, C4) Snazzy microbrewery and restaurant mainly populated with locals of all ages. The windows and interior are adorned with numerous vintage brewery artefacts and a pair of gleaming copper vats, though it's the unusual house beers – including coffee, banana and champagne varieties – that really draw the crowds here.
☎ 296 216 666
🖥 www.gastroinfo.cz/pivodum ✉ Lípová 15 (entry on Ječná), Nové Město ☽ 11am-11.30pm
Ⓜ IP Pavlova

Propaganda (4, C6) This small, busy neighbourhood pub, strewn with abstract sculptures, attracts a youngish crowd, half of whom seem to gather permanently around the table-football in the back room. Accepts euros.
☎ 224 932 285
🖥 www.volny.cz/propagandabar
✉ Pštrossova 29, Nové Město ☽ 3pm-2am Mon-Fri, 5pm-2am Sat-Sun
Ⓜ Národní Třída

Rocky O'Reilly's (4, F6) No prizes for guessing, yes this is an Irish pub (they serve

Absinthe Makes the Heart Grow Fonder

Actually, absinthe rots the brain thanks to its wormwood flavouring, or at least this was the consensus that led to the banning of the 'green fairy' (70% alcohol content) across Europe in the early 20th century after many years of vigorous consumption, particularly in France. As is the case in times of prohibition, though, this often just increased the forbidden appeal of absinthe (*absinth* in Czech), particularly to literate drunks like Ernest Hemingway.

The concoction was outlawed in Czechoslovakia during the communist era, but was legalised again in the 1990s after being re-adopted by Czech trendsetters, who strangely believed that acquiring an epic hangover gave them anti-establishment kudos.

Guinness and have photos of James Joyce and Bernard Shaw on the wall). It's a popular with the boisterous Brit and Irish crowd. There's live sport on satellite TV, and a separate restaurant serving excellent value 'pub grub' (p71).
🖥 www.rockyoreillys.cz
✉ Štěpánská 32, Nové Město ☽ 10am-1am
Ⓜ Muzeum

The Thirsty Dog (4, D2)
Not exactly the place to discuss Descartes over a daiquiri, but this is still a very popular hang out for the Anglo backpacker set. There's a pool table, comfy seating and Sky Sports on tap to keep patrons entertained. They also serve filling English breakfasts and slightly less filling snack food.
☎ 222 310 039 ✉ Elišky Krásnohrské 5, Josefov
☽ 11am-2am Mon-Fri, noon-2am Sat-Sun
Ⓜ Staroměstská

Tlustá Koala (4, F3)
Friendly, British-style pub, complete with dartboards, hunting prints, and lots of polished wood and brass. Surprisingly, most of the clientele are locals, though. You can take a seat outside, but the view isn't exactly fantastic, there's also a restaurant in the back serving traditional Czech food.
☎ 222 245 401
🖥 www.a-tlustakoala.com ✉ Senovážná 8, Nové Město ☽ noon-1am Ⓜ Náměestí Republiky

Glittering, gleaming microbrewery, Pivovarský Dům

Tlustá Myš (4, A5)
The subterranean 'Fat Mouse' pub is very much a local bar, with a couple of small rooms with long tables for those sociable evening drinks. The extensive list of inventive cocktails may keep you longer than you anticipated, and there are also very small exhibitions of local art.
☎ 605 282 506
✉ Všehrdova 19, Malá Strana ☽ 11am-midnight Mon-Thu, 2pm-1am Fri-Sat, 3-11pm Sun Ⓜ Anděl

U Osla v Kolébce (5, B3)
This quiet little pub shares a secluded courtyard with 'Kelly's Tower'. Curious about the pub's unusual name? 'The Donkey in the Cradle' comes from a local legend that involved Kelly cursing a woman by turning her baby's head (temporarily, thankfully) into that of an ass. If the sun is shining, make use of the outside tables.
☎ 777 250 526
✉ Jánský vršek 8, Malá Strana ☽ 11am-11pm
Ⓜ Malostranská

Now what did they say to drink at Tlustá Koala?

CLUBS

Futurum (6, B4) Has record launches, alternative bands and various DJs in attendance but mostly it's a case of back to the future (lots of metal, exposed brick walls and weird lighting), with '80s and '90s music. ☎ 257 328 571 🖳 www .musicbar.cz ✉ Zborovská 7, Smíchov 💲 100Kč 🕑 8pm-3am Ⓜ Anděl

Garáž (5, C3) Spirited two-level bar/club downstairs at Jo's, usually well-patronised by chatter-hungry expats and backpackers until the wee hours, with a peak in attendance during Happy Hour (6-10pm) ☎ 257 533 342 ✉ Malostranské náměstí 7, Malá Strana 💲 free 🕑 6pm-5am Ⓜ Malostranská

Joshua Tree (7, F2) U2-inspired subterranean Irish bar/club/restaurant with regular live bands (Thu), as well as top Czech and international guest DJs (Wed, Fri & Sat). Runs summer-only beer-garden in the Slovanský Dům courtyard. ☎ 221 451 271 🖳 www.joshuatree.cz

Even the DJ is slick at fashionable Radost FX

✉ Slovanský Dům, Na příkopě 22, Staré Město 💲 free 🕑 restaurant/bar 11am-2am, shows 10pm-late Ⓜ Náměstí Republiky

Karlovy Lázně (4, C4) Four-level 'superclub' where you can watch live bands at ground level (MCM Café), boogie on 1 (Discothéque), shuffle to the top 10 on 2 (Kaleidoskop), or bypass them all and head for the solid drum'n'bass and break beat on 3 (Paradogs). ☎ 222 220 502 🖳 www.karlovylazne.cz ✉ Novotného lávka, Staré Město 💲 50-100Kč 🕑 9pm-5am Ⓜ Staroměstská

Mecca (6, D2) This ultra-fashionable hang out is all stark colours, space-age vinyl couches, and the sorts of chairs that challenge you to try and sit on them. Fashion people, models and their followers flock to Mecca's industrial-chic club to dance to house, drum'n'bass and techno. ☎ 283 870 522 🖳 www.mecca.cz ✉ U Průhonu, Holešovice 💲 150-200Kč 🕑 11am-10pm Mon-Thu, 11am-6am Fri (club from 10pm), noon-6am Sat (club from 10pm) Ⓜ Nádraží Holešovice

Meloun (7, C4) This dark cellar bar and club attracts a largely local, youthful crowd, especially for the weekend Czech pop discos, when you'll be lucky to squeeze through the door. Western pop plays on Mondays, while Tuesday is karaoke night. ☎ 224 230 126 🖳 www.meloun.cz ✉ Michalská 12, Staré Město 💲 Mon, Wed &

Thu free, Tue 60Kč, Fri-Sat 90Kč ⌚ 7pm-3am Mon-Sat Ⓜ Můstek

Radost FX (3, A2) Prague's slickest, shiniest and most self-assured club. Its bohemian lounge is appealingly decked out in mosaic-topped tables and sumptuous chaises longues, while the downstairs club draws the city's beautiful people to groove along to house and funk. Yeah baby. ☎ 224 254 776 🖳 www.radostfx.cz ✉ Bělehradská 120, Vinohrady 💲 100-250Kč ⌚ lounge 11am-4am, club 10pm-6am Ⓜ IP Pavlova

Roxy (4, F2) The expansive floor of this iconic, ramshackle old theatre has seen many a hard-edged DJ and band over the years, plus plenty of experimental fare in the form of drama, dance and short films. All shadowy nooks and crannies usually fill up quickly once the doors open.

☎ 224 826 390 🖳 www .roxy.cz ✉ Dlouhá 33, Josefov 💲 50-250Kč (Mon free) ⌚ 8pm-late Ⓜ Náměstí Republiky

Solidní nejistota (4, C6) Catering to the over-25 crowd, Solidní nejistota ('Solid Uncertainty') has a red interior allegedly inspired by Uluru in Australia, and rotating exhibitions of paintings by young local artists. There are live, and diverse, bands nightly, and snack dishes like marinated sheep's cheese and smoked meat plates. ☎ 224 933 086 ✉ Pštrossova 21, Nové

Město 💲 free ⌚ 5pm-6am Ⓜ Národní Třída

Stromovka Music Garden (6, C2) This is basically a big beer garden with a stage beside the Fairgrounds, attracting a wide array of acts and DJs, and an almost entirely local audience. Relax with a glass of Gambrinus under the trees and tap your foot to anything from klezmer to '80s party music. 🖳 www.stromovka .com ✉ areál Výstaviště, Holešovice 💲 50-100Kč ⌚ 10am-3am, shows from 7pm Ⓜ Nádraží Holešovice

Radost FX has the atmosphere, the style and the music to make for a top place to be

JAZZ

AghaRTA Jazz Centrum (4, F6) Since 1991 this club has been staging top-notch modern Czech jazz, blues, funk and fusion in its humbly furnished auditorium. Don't worry if you turn up and no one else is there – the audience will drift in about 30mins before showtime. Check out the CD counter (p55) for some great jazz buys.

☎ 222 211 275
🖳 www.agharta.cz
✉ Krakovská 5, Nové Město ⑤ 100Kč ⏱ 7pm-1am, shows 9pm-midnight Ⓜ Muzeum

Jazz Boat (4, D1) This vessel's 2½hr Vltava-cruising concerts are pitched forcefully at tourists, but some popular local outfits perform here. Its 'restaurant' offers unremarkable food and beverage at extra cost.

☎ 603 551 680
🖳 www.jazzboat.cz
✉ Pier No 5, under

If you like your jazz intimate, get to Reduta Jazz Club

Čechův most, Josefov ⑤ 590Kč ⏱ 8.30-11pm Tue-Sun Ⓜ Staroměstská

Jazz Club Železná (7, D3) Smoky subterranean venue with a wonderfully innovative program of jazz, swing and blues. A mixed crowd of locals and travellers regularly pack it to its stone vaulted ceiling. There's occasional open-mic poetry and a small shop selling 2nd-hand CDs.

☎ 224 239 697
✉ Železná 16, Staré Město ⑤ 120Kč in

advance, 150Kč on the door ⏱ 3pm-1am, shows 9pm-midnight Ⓜ Můstek

Metropolitan Jazz Club (4, E6) Basement jazz'n'blues haunt, with easily digestible ragtime and swing compositions. There's a preference for substance over style, hence the plain-tiled floor and general lack of adornment.

☎ 224 947 777
✉ Jungmannova 14, Nové Město ⑤ 100Kč ⏱ 6pm-1am Mon-Fri, 7pm-1am Sat-Sun; shows 9pm-12.30am Ⓜ Národní Třída

Reduta (4, D5) Intimate jazz setting, with well-attired patrons squeezing into tiered seats and lounges to soak up the big-band, swing and dixieland atmosphere. Occasionally oversells tickets, causing a last-minute scramble for seating.

☎ 224 933 487 🖳 www.redutajazzclub.cz
✉ Národní 20, Nové Město ⑤ 280-300Kč ⏱ box office from 3pm Mon-Fri, from 7pm

Playing Solo

Entertaining your sole self in Prague is easy and uncomplicated. Cafes and bars are invariably dotted with unaccompanied Czechs and foreigners enjoying their own company or the qualities of a good book, newspaper or menu, while live music venues also have their share of self-possessed attendees.

Though wandering into a crowded beer hall on your own may at first appear an intimidating exercise, just head for a space at a less-populated bench and inquire *'Je tu volno'* ('Is it free?') before sitting down. You may even find yourself waved over to a spare spot with companionable, refreshment-flowing consequences.

Sat-Sun; shows 9.30pm-midnight ⓜ Národní Třída

U Malého Glena (5, C4)
Melange of jazz styles (and blues) served up nightly in this informal venue, including modern, latin and vocal. Jam sessions are regularly held here – amateurs welcome!
☎ 257 531 717
🖥 www.malyglen.cz
✉ Karmelitská 23, Malá Strana $ 100-150Kč 🕑 10am-2am; shows 9.30pm-12.30am ⓜ Malostranská

Ungelt Jazz & Blues Club (7, D2) This popular, if poky, 15th-century vault venue can be crammed with people attracted by 'Free Jazz' signage around the Old Town Square, but it appears an admission price is usually charged. Jazz fusion and blues dominate the nightly program. Nice!
☎ 224 895 748
🖥 www.jazzblues.cz
✉ Týnská ulička 2, Staré Město $ 120Kč 🕑 pub noon-midnight, jazz club 8pm-late, shows 9pm-midnight ⓜ Náměstí Republiky

U Staré Paní (7, C4)
Located in the bowels of the hotel of the same name, this well-established jazz club caters to all levels of musical appreciation. There's a varied program of modern jazz, soul, blues and

U Staré Paní jazz club

latin rhythms, and a nightly DJ spot from midnight on.
☎ 603 551 680 🖥 www.jazzinprague.com
✉ Michalská 9, Staré Město $ 150Kč 🕑 7pm-2am, shows 9pm- midnight, 'World Music Party' from midnight ⓜ Můstek

ROCK, BLUES & FOLK

Dlabačov Hall (6, A3)
The Czech Song and Dance Ensemble, formed in 1947, is the republic's sole professional folk performance troupe, though other 'folklore' events are irregularly and mostly less impressively staged elsewhere by private companies.
☎ 233 373 475 ✉ Hotel Pyramida, Bělohorská 24, Střešovice $ 450Kč 🕑 shows 8.30pm Mon-Sat Apr-Nov ⓜ Hradčanská, then tram 8 to Malovanka

Klub 007 (6, A3) Not exactly the kind of place Bond, James Bond, might frequent. This grungy student hang out in an inconspicuous location under the stairs on the eastern side of dorm block 7, plays very, very loud punk, death metal, jungle and hip-hop.
☎ 257 211 439 🖥 www.klub007strahov.cz
✉ Block 7, Strahov dormitory complex, Chaloupekého 7, Strahov $ 120Kč 🕑 7.30pm-1am Tue-Sat, shows 8pm ⓜ Dejvická, then bus 143, 149 or 217 to Chaloupekého

Lucerna Music Bar (4, F5)
Nostalgia rules at this atmospheric old theatre, with anything from a Beatles covers band to Czech blues, rock or folk acts on stage. 1980s and '90s 'video parties' are particularly popular, while other random offerings include 1960s Czech pop and 1950s Americana.
☎ 224 217 108
🖥 www.musicbar.cz
✉ Lucerna Passage, Vodičkova 36, Nové Město

Lucerna Music Bar

$ 50-150Kč ☻ 8pm-4am, shows from 9pm Ⓜ Muzeum

Malostranská beseda (5, C3) The unpretentious upstairs environs of the former town hall of Malá Strana is now favoured by Czechs of all ages for its nightly agenda of rock, jazz, folk and country music performers. Packs out early, particularly on weekends. ☎ 257 532 092 ✉ Malostranské náměstí 21, Malá Strana $ 80-100Kč ☻ bar 5pm-1am, shows 8.30pm Ⓜ Malostranská

Palác Akropolis (6, D3) Labyrinthine entertainment palace with a wealth of alternative talent (local and international) on show in its various performance spaces, from Macedonian gypsy bands to string quartets and hip-hop. Has a good cafe and restaurant too. ☎ 296 330 911 🖥 www .palacakropolis.cz ✉ Kubelíkova 27, Žižkov $ 150-300Kč ☻ cafe 10am-midnight Mon-Fri, 4pm-midnight Sat-Sun; club 4pm-4am Ⓜ Jiřího z Poděbrad

Red Hot & Blues (7, F1) More Tex-Mex dinner show than blues bar or jazz joint, but still pleases the out-of-towners with its mixture of live music and platefuls of Creole and Cajun cooking. The courtyard is a great place to raise a glass to a Lazy Pigs Hillbilly Blues Band number. ☎ 222 314 639 ✉ Jakubská 12, Staré Město $ free ☻ 9am-11pm, shows 7-10pm Ⓜ Náměstí Republiky

Rock Café (4, D5) Over-commercialised to the hilt and loving it, there's a cinema, art gallery and an auditorium. Check out 'Free Puerto' night (Tue in summer), a blend of bhangra, flamenco, reggae and 'songs of Mongolian herdsmen'. ☎ 224 933 947 🖥 www .rockcafe.cz ✉ Národní 20, Nové Město $ 50-100Kč ☻ 10am-3am Mon-Fri, 5pm-3am Sat, 5pm-1am Sun; shows 8.30pm Ⓜ Národní Třída

THEATRE

All Colours Theatre (7, D3) One of Prague's top black-light theatre exponents, putting on bizarre and colourful shows with outstanding special effects accompanying the music and dancing. During the break they'll give you a tour of the gallery. ☎ 221 610 114 🖥 www .blacktheatre.cz ✉ Rytířská 31, Nové Město $ 490Kč ☻ 8.30pm; box office 10am-9pm Ⓜ Můstek ♿

Celetná Theatre (7, E2) In an arcade running between Celetná and Štupartská, the Divadlo v Celetné is the dramatic abode of the industrious Jiří Srnec Black Light Theatre of Prague. Book ahead. ☎ 222 326 843 🖥 www .divadlovceletne.cz ✉ Celetná 17, Staré Město $ up to 250Kč, ☻ usually at least 1 show daily at 7.30pm; box office 1-7.30pm Ⓜ Náměstí Republiky ♿

Goja Music Hall (6, C2) Striking glass pyramid-shaped theatre in the Fairgrounds hosting conventional international shows and hit musicals such as Les Misérables (in Czech). ☎ 272 658 955 🖥 www .goja.cz ✉ Fairgrounds (Výstaviště), Holešovice $ 649Kč Ⓜ Nádraží Holešovice, then tram 5, 12, 17, 53 or 54 to Výstaviště ♿

Image Theatre (7, C2) Creative black-light theatre, with pantomime, contemporary dance and video – not to mention liberal doses of slapstick – to tell their stories. The staging can be very effective, but the atmosphere is often dictated by audience reaction. ☎ 222 314 448 🖥 www.imagetheatre.cz ✉ Pařížská 4, Staré Město $ 400Kč ☻ performances 8pm; box office 9am-8pm Ⓜ Staroměstská

Laterna Magika (4, C5) Since its first cutting-edge show, an amalgamated stage performance with music, dance and film at the 1958 Brussels World

Fair, Laterna Magika has been highly successful both at home and abroad, and now commands the New National Theatre building. The mix of live dance and projected images continues to draw the crowds.

☎ 224 931 482 ▢ www.laterna.cz ✉ Národní 4, Nové Město $ 680Kč ☙ performances 8pm Mon-Sat; box office 10am-8pm Mon-Sat Ⓜ Národní Třída

Laterna Magika in the new National Theatre building

National Marionette Theatre (7, B2)

Loudly touted as the longest-running classical marionette show in the city, *Don Giovanni* is an operatic, life-sized marionette extravaganza that has spawned several imitators around town. Younger kids' interests may begin to wane quite early during this 2hr show.

☎ 224 819 323 ▢ www.mozart.cz ✉ Žatecká 1, Staré Město $ 490/390Kč ☙ performances 8pm;

box office 10am-8pm Ⓜ Staroměstská ♿

Spiral Theatre (6, C2)

In the sprawling Fairgrounds in Holešovice, this tall black industrial rotunda of a building hosts various shows, including productions of Shakespeare and local and international music acts.

☎ 220 103 624 ✉ Fairgrounds (Výstaviště), Holešovice $ 200-495Kč ☙ box office 3-7pm Tue-Sun Ⓜ Nádraží Holešovice, then tram 5, 12, 17, 53 or 54 to Výstaviště

Theatre on the Balustrade (7, A4)

Immerse yourself in Czech-language drama at the theatre where Václav Havel honed his skills as a playwright four decades ago. This 'off-Národní' theatre (Divadlo Na zábradlí) dabbled in absurdism early in its existence and now plays host to a variety of slightly more contemporary material.

☎ 222 222 026 ▢ www.nazabradli.cz ✉ Anenské náměstí 5, Staré Město $ 90-250Kč ☙ box office 2-7pm Ⓜ Staroměstská ♿

Glowing Acts

Contrary to what you might think, 'black-light theatre' does not involve sitting in a hall with the lights turned off, or an experimental play by astrophysicists featuring collapsed stars. Rather, it's a mixture of mime, dance, drama and puppetry performed in front of a black backdrop by ultraviolet-illuminated actors and objects all dressed in phosphorescent garb.

A growing number of places are presenting this theatrical genre in Prague. The more interesting and entertaining companies include the Jiří Srnec Black Light Theatre of Prague (p88), Image Theatre (p88) and All Colours Theatre (p88).

CLASSICAL MUSIC, OPERA & BALLET

Bertramka (6, A4) Mozart stayed in this restored villa during his visits to Prague, and it is now a museum and charming venue for classical concerts, held in the salon and gardens. String quartets, wind trios and so on provide the notes.
☎ 257 318 461
💻 www.bertramka
.cz ✉ Mozartova 169, Smíchov 💲 350-565Kč
🕑 5pm & 7pm Apr-Oct
Ⓜ Anděl then tram 10 to Kartouzská

Estates Theatre (7, D3) This Stavovské Divadlo is the oldest theatre in Prague, famed as the place where Mozart conducted the premiere of *Don Giovanni*, a touristy version of which is staged by the Opera Mozart company each summer. The rest of the year sees various operatic and ballet productions.
☎ 224 901 638
✉ Ovocný trh 1, Staré

Město 💲 190-1950Kč
🕑 box office (in Kolow-rat Palace, Ovocný trh 6 10am-6pm Mon-Fri, 10am-12.30pm Sat-Sun; evening box office in theatre open 30mins before performances Ⓜ Můstek
♿ good, plus facilities for the hearing-impaired

Municipal House (7, F2) Smetana Hall, centrepiece of the stunning Obecní Dům, is the city's biggest concert hall with a capacity of 1500. This is where you can catch the Prague Symphony Orchestra and musical stage shows such as *Rockquiem* (a 'Rock' version of Mozart's *Requiem*). Other halls host regular recitals, from Gershwin to Bach.
☎ 222 002 101 💻 www .fok.cz ✉ náměstí Republiky 5, Staré Město
💲 200-1200Kč 🕑 box office (U Obecního domu 2) 10am-6pm & 1hr before concerts Mon-Fri
Ⓜ Náměstí Republiky

National Theatre (4, C5) Glorious, golden-roofed centrepiece of Czech performing arts institutions, Národní Divadlo is credited with providing a forum for the emancipation of Czech culture. Traditional opera, drama and ballet performances by the likes of Tchaikovsky, Smetana and Shakespeare share the stage with more modern works by Philip Glass, John Osborne and others.
☎ 114 901 448
💻 www.narodni-divadlo.cz ✉ Národní 2, Nové Město 💲 310-930Kč 🕑 box office 10am-6pm; evening box office in theatre open 45mins before performances Ⓜ Národní Třída

Prague State Opera (4, G5) The impressive neo-rococo home of the Prague State Opera (Státní Opera Praha) is a glorious setting for operatic standards and

Just the Ticket

Even up to 30 minutes before a performance starts, you can often still get a ticket at the box office. When booking ahead is advised or you have your rear end primed for a particular seat, the following computerised ticket agencies can help you out – note that you're probably looking at a 10-15% mark-up and some agencies don't take credit cards.

Bohemia Ticket (7, C3; ☎ 224 227 832; fax 224 218 167; 💻 www.bohemia ticket.cz; Malé náměstí 13, Staré Město)

Ticketpro (7, C1; ☎ 224 816 020; 💻 www.ticketpro.cz; Salvátorská 10, Josefov; closed Sat-Sun) or (7, D4; ☎ 221 610 162; Řytířská 12, Staré Město; open every day)

FOK (mainly Prague Symphony Orchestra tickets; 7, F2; ☎ 222 002 336; 💻 www.fok.cz; U Obecního domu 2, Nové Město)

the occasional ballet. The annual Verdi Festival takes place in Aug/Sep, while less conventional recent productions have included Scott Joplin's *Treemonisha* and Leoncavallo's rarely-staged version of *La Bohème*.
☎ 224 227 832
🖳 www.opera.cz
✉ Wilsonova 4, Nové Město 💲 opera 400-1200Kč, ballet 200-550Kč; reductions for some matinées 🕑 box office 10am-5.30pm Mon-Fri, 10am-noon & 1-5.30pm Sat-Sun Ⓜ Muzeum

Rudolfinum (4, C2)

Within the massive neo-Renaissance Rudolfinum you'll find the colonnade-lined Dvořák Hall. This magnificent concert hall is the performance base for the world-renowned Czech Philharmonic Orchestra. Simply sit back and be impressed by some of the best classical musicians in Prague.
☎ 227 059 352 🖳 www .czechphilharmonic.cz
✉ náměstí Jana Palacha 1, Josefov 💲 150-900Kč, concession available most shows 🕑 box office 10am-6pm & 1hr before concerts Mon-Fri Ⓜ Staroměstská

Villa Amerika (6, C4)

Villa Amerika was built in 1717 as a count's immodest summer retreat. These days it's the home of the Dvořák Museum and its salon is used by the Original Music Theatre of Prague as a historical setting for their

State Opera House

period-costumed vocal and instrumental show, *Wonderful Dvořák*.
☎ 224 918 013 14
✉ Ke Karlovu 20, Nové Město 💲 545Kč 🕑 8pm Tue & Fri Apr-Oct Ⓜ IP Pavlova

CINEMAS

Jalta (4, F5)

Usually shows a couple of English-language flicks subtitled in Czech, convenient for when you need some respite from the commercial scramble on Wenceslas Square.
☎ 224 228 814
🖳 www.djg.cz/jalta
✉ Václavské náměstí 43, Nové Město 💲 70-95Kč 🕑 box office open from 3pm Ⓜ Muzeum

Kino 64 U Hradeb (5, C4)

On the edge of a decorous courtyard with a dry fountain behind Maccas, this cinema shows the more mainstream foreign-language films, accompanied by on-screen Czech translations.
☎ 257 531 158
✉ Mostecká 21, Malá Strana 💲 110-180Kč
🕑 box office 2-9.30pm
Ⓜ Malostranská

Kino Perštýn (4, D5)

Downstairs cinema that forgoes those boring old rows of seats for a sociable scattering of tables and chairs. You can smoke in the next-door bar, but only drinks (and not fumes) can accompany you into the cinema. English/foreign-language films with Czech subtitles.
☎ 221 668 432 ✉ Na Perstýně 6, Staré Město 💲 80-130Kč

🕑 box office from 4pm
Ⓜ Národní Třída

Kotva – Broadway (7, F1)

Compact seven-row theatre on the ground floor of

Cinema poster advertising

Kotva, screening a mix of mainstream English and foreign-language films, mostly with Czech subtitles, although some are dubbed.
☎ 224 828 316
✉ náměstí Republiky 8, Staré Město $ 80-100Kč
🕐 box office 10.30-11.30am & 1.30-11.30pm
Ⓜ Náměstí Republiky

Lucerna (4, F5)
There's a limited selection of motion pictures at this one-theatre venue, but it exudes a demi-monde charm, and you have to admit there's a certain novelty in asking your friends to meet you under the upside-down horse (p34).
☎ 224 216 972
✉ Lucerna Passage, Vodičkova 36, Nové Město
$ 110Kč 🕐 box office 10am-noon, 1-7.30pm, 8-9.15pm Ⓜ Muzeum

MAT Studio (6, C4)
Former TV studio and private screening venue turned cool cinema, where film types sip espressos

Palace Cinema advertises its 10 screens of movies

and wine in the celluloid-decorated downstairs bar/club or the arty upstairs bistro. Czech films with English subtitles and vice versa.
☎ 224 915 765 🖥 www .mat.cz ✉ Karlovo náměstí 19, Nové Město
$ 60-100Kč 🕐 11am-midnight Mon-Fri , 2pm-midnight Sat-Sun
Ⓜ Karlovo Náměstí ♿

Palace Cinema (7, F3)
Ten screens of big-budget, Western-style entertainment in one brightly lit complex. Plays mainstream movies, but history buffs can also see a 50min film on the city's past, *Prague 1000 Years* (all tickets 99Kč).
☎ 257 181 212 🖥 www .palacecinemas.cz ✉ Na příkopě 22, Nové Město
$ 150/99Kč 🕐 box office 11.30am-9pm Mon-Fri, 11.30am-10.30pm Sat-Sun Ⓜ Náměstí Republiky ♿

Moving Pictures

Czech filmmaking blossomed from 1963-68, when graduates of a Communist-run film academy side-stepped censorship. Among them was Miloš Forman, who produced 1963's *Černý Petr* (Black Peter). Jan Svěrák directed two pivotal films: *Kolja* (1996), about a Russian boy reared by a Czech man; and *Tmavomodrý svět* (The Dark-Blue World; 2001), concerning Czech pilots in WWII. David Ondříček released the acclaimed *Samotáři* in 2000, a year that also saw Jan Hrebejk's Academy Award-nominated *Musíme si pomáhat* (Divided We Fall).

International flicks that have been substantially shot in the Czech capital include Forman's *Amadeus*, Barbara Streisand's *Yentl* and Brian de Palma's *Mission Impossible*. Shooting began on Terry Gilliam's *Brothers Grimm*, starring Matt Damon, in 2003.

GAY & LESBIAN PRAGUE

A-Club (6, D3) This highly rated late-night lesbian bar is tucked away in the back-blocks of Žižkov. Friday night is for women only, while both Friday and Saturday nights are regularly enlivened by a disco.
☎ 222 781 623
✉ Miličova 25, Žižkov
$ Sun-Thu free, Fri 25Kč, Sat 50Kč ☽ 7pm-6am Ⓜ Jiřího z Poděbrad

Babylonia (4, D5) Gay-only sauna which extends itself beyond steam and hot rocks to provide a Jacuzzi, fitness room and massages. To help you achieve a balance between your health-oriented goals and your less-salubrious impulses, there's also a bar.
☎ 224 232 304
✉ Martinská 6, Staré Město $ 200Kč ☽ 2pm-3am Ⓜ Národní Třída

Escape (4, C4) One of the flashiest gay clubs on the Prague block, amalgamating a late-night restaurant with go-go dancers and a vividly dressed disco. Not to be confused with the cocktail bar of the same name in the Old Town.
☎ 606 538 111
🖳 www.volny.cz/escapeclub ✉ V Jámě 8, Nové Město ☽ 8pm-5am Ⓜ Národní Třída

Friends (4, C4) Good cellar spot to sit back and sip some wine or coffee, or to join in the busy spirit of assorted theme nights. These can include Czech music, movies or hits of the '60s; DJs add their own spin from 10pm.
☎ 221 635 4 08
🖳 www.friends-prague.cz ✉ Náprstkova 1, Staré Město ☽ 4pm-3am Ⓜ Národní Třída

Gejzeer (3, C1) Large gay and lesbian club that draws an equally large crowd to its dual bars and disco. Besides the usual dance and video-related activities, Gejzeer seems keen to play matchmaker by offering 'meet a partner' nights and its equally euphemistic 'darkroom'.
☎ 222 516 036
🖳 www.volny.cz/gejzeer

✉ Vinohradská 40, Vinohrady $ Thu free, Fri & Sat free to 10.30pm then 50-70Kč ☽ 8pm-4am Thu, 9pm-5am Fri, 9pm-6am Sat Ⓜ Náměstí Míru

Pinocchio (6, D3) Sizeable confluence of gay clubbers with a lively gambling room, strip-show-enhanced bar, and a very popular disco that leaves you with a neon afterglow. Upstairs is a gay hotel (separate entry) with a dozen basic but well-maintained rooms.
☎ 222 710 773
🖳 www.volny.cz/pinocchio ✉ Seifertova 3, Žižkov $ free ☽ 3pm-6am Ⓜ Hlavní Nádraží

Pivnice U Rudolfa (4, F6) Intimate gay beer hall with cosy subterranean surrounds, just a brief stroll from the Muzeum metro. It's popular with older locals during the day, and then gets considerably livelier late at night.
☎ 0604 58 51 53
✉ Mezibranská 3, Nové Město $ free ☽ 4pm-2am Ⓜ Muzeum

SPORT

Prague International Marathon

The annual 42km Prague International Marathon first hit the streets in 1989 and now attracts more foreigners than locals. The full run – from Old Town Square around Josefov, over Charles Bridge, south down Malá Strana and then back up to the square – is usually staged in the latter half of May, and a half-marathon is held mid-March. If you fancy your chances, the times to beat are 2:26:33 for women and 2:08:52 for men.

Ice Hockey

Czechs love ice hockey *(lední hokey)*. They've won 10 world titles, most recently in 2001. There are 14 teams in the national league, including the successful Sparta Praha and Slavia Praha, but for several years the competition has been a one-puck race led by a team from Vsetin. Catch the action at T-Mobile Arena.

Football

In August-December and February-June, AC Sparta Praha competes with itself to see how many points clear at the top of the ladder it will be by the domestic season's end. Although this team is occasionally pressed by rivals, it usually makes a lot of vocal football *(fotbal)* followers ecstatic by the competition's end. Catch a game at the AC Sparta Praha stadium.

Horse Racing

If racing *(dostihy)* is your scene, head down to the horse-pounded turf at Chuchle závodiště. Races are generally run between April and November, on Sunday from 2pm onwards. The inexpensive tickets should be available at the racecourse *(závodiště)*. If you fancy a flutter, the minimum stake is 20Kč.

Offices & Venues

- **Prague International Marathon** (4, F7; ☎ 224 919 209; 🖳 www.pim.cz; 5th fl, Záhořanského 3, Nové Město; Ⓜ Karlovo náměstí)
- **HC Sparta Praha** (6, C2; ☎ 266 727 421; 🖳 www.hcsparta.cz; T-Mobile Arena, Za Elektrárnou 419, Bubeneč; Ⓜ Nádraží Holešovice then tram 5, 12, 17, 53 or 54 to Výstaviště)
- **AC Sparta Praha stadium** (6, B2; ☎ 220 570 323; 🖳 www .sparta.cz; Milady Horákové 98, Bubeneč; Ⓜ Hradčanská then tram 1, 8, 25, 26, 51 or 56)
- **Chuchle závodiště** (6, B6; ☎ 257 941 431; 🖳 www.velka-chuchle.cz; Radotínská 69, Velká Chuchle; Ⓜ Smíchovské Nádraží then bus 129 or 172 to Chuchle závodiště)

Sleeping

Prague is inundated with visitors year-round but the busiest time is between April and October, and particularly over Easter, Christmas and New Year, when they eagerly consume large portions of the available accommodation. It's better to book your lodgings as far ahead as possible during these times, and when your trip coincides with local and European public holidays.

The terms 'budget accommodation' and 'city centre' are almost mutually exclusive in Prague, bar a few cheap hostels and hotels within camera-lens distance of Old Town Square. The majority of budget places, where you'll usually find crowded dorms or ultra-plain rooms with shared bathroom, are scattered outside Staré Město – most are in southern Nové Město, east in Vinohrady, and north across the Vltava in Holešovice. Many *penzións* (pensions), traditionally private boarding houses, can turn out to be hotels attempting a mum-and-dad appeal – some of the genuine ones have homey surrounds, though these tend to be in outer areas.

> ### Room Rates
>
> The prices in this chapter indicate the cost per night of a standard double room in high season.
>
> | | |
> |---|---|
> | Deluxe | over 7500Kč |
> | Top End | 5500-7500Kč |
> | Mid-Range | 2500-5499Kč |
> | Budget | under 2500Kč |

Mid-range options are often three-star hotels (star ratings are self-applied) with their own restaurant, cafe and/or bar, and rooms equipped with bathroom, satellite TV, phone and minibar; some places overcharge foreigners for poorly maintained premises. Meanwhile, there's no shortage of top-end choices stuffed full of classy eateries, grand fittings and business facilities.

A growing trend involves inner-city dwellers doing apartment renovations (sometimes minimalist) and then renting them to travellers for short or long-term stays. If you go for a flat in the more trampled bits of the Old Town, make sure your bedroom isn't facing the street – late-night revellers tend to treat the narrow streets as their own private karaoke studio. And when inquiring about apartments, take a good hard look at the location, as many are right out in the suburbs. If you want to do your own leg-work, head out to your preferred area and look for signs saying *privát* or *Zimmer frei* (rooms for rent).

Note that many hotels, especially in the upper-end bracket, quote prices in euros, and even though the Czech Republic is not a member of the eurozone, you can still pay in the currency.

DELUXE

Four Seasons Hotel (7, A2) An executive villa for all seasons beside the Vltava offering some of the largest suites in Prague. Internet access, massage on call and a health club for adults and video games, bedtime milk and cookies and mini-bathrobes for the kids. Under-18s stay free in their parents' room.
☎ 221 427 000
🖳 www.fourseasons .com/prague ✉ Vele-slavínova 2a, Staré Město Ⓜ Staroměstská ✖ Allegro ♿

Grand Hotel Bohemia (7, F2) It may have an antique exterior and a neobaroque ballroom, but this is a thoroughly modern member of an Austrian hotel chain, with efficient service and spacious, if business-like, rooms. Kids 7-12 years of age are charged 50% less; children under six stay free of charge.

☎ 234 608 111
🖳 www.grandhotelbohe mia.cz ✉ Králodvorsk 4, Staré Město Ⓜ Náměstí Republiky ✖

Hotel Josef (4, F2) With a stark white, minimalist vestibule more reminiscent of an exclusive Swiss clinic than a luxury hotel, this striking designer place has 110 sound-proof rooms, many non-smoking, and two for disabled guests. Also has a bar and business lounge, and the grooviest glass spiral staircase around.
☎ 221 700 111
🖳 www.hoteljosef.com ✉ Rybná 70, Staré Město Ⓜ Náměstí Republiky ✖ Byblos (p72)

Hotel Hoffmeister (4, B1) Named after celebrity-loving caricaturist Adolf Hoffmeister, whose work adorns a gallery here. Like the hotel generally, rooms can be a bit stuffy and overdressed

Art Nouveau Hotel Paříž

(with a preponderance of swags, chunky furniture and fussy decorations) but staff are very attentive and the old castle steps conveniently beckon nearby.
☎ 251 017 111
🖳 www.hoffmeister.cz ✉ Pod Bruskou 7, Hradčany Ⓜ Malostran-ská ✖ Ada

Hotel Paříž (7, F2) Bastion of Art Nouveau grandeur circa 1904, now with essential 21st-century mod-cons

The glass spiral staircase in minimalist lobby of Hotel Josef is an entry into luxury

like heated bathroom floors and massage facilities. Rooms have the requisite bygone era trimmings but remain plushly modern. If you're not staying here, poke your head into the elegant stairwell to see its hand-painted motifs.
☎ 222 195 195
🖳 www.hotel-pariz.cz
✉ U Obecního domu 1, Staré Město Ⓜ Malostranská, then tram 22 or 23 to Pohořelec ✖ Restaurant Sarah Bernhardt (p75); Café de Paris ⚖

Hotel Questenberk (2, B2)
Opened in a baroque 17th-century former church hospital in 2003, Questenberk is certainly one of Prague's unique hotels, within strolling distance of the Castle and Strahov Monastery. The calm, church-like atmosphere has been retained, with added mod-cons like satellite TV and modem connections.
☎ 220 407 600
🖳 www.questenberk.cz
✉ Úvoz 15, Hradčany Ⓜ Malostranská ✖ Malý Buddha (p63) ⚖

Hotel Savoy (2, A2) Has appropriately elegant rooms, plus a leather-bound library and a sky-lit restaurant. It caters to the stressed traveller by providing fitness trainers, hairdressers, a sauna and a gym. It is, however, a little far from the centre of things.
☎ 224 302 430 🖳 www.hotel-savoy.cz ✉ Keplerova 6, Hradčany Ⓜ Malostranská ✖ U Labutí (p63) ⚖

The Radisson SAS Alcron is as popular as ever

Radisson SAS Alcron Hotel (4, F6) Luxury five-star Art Deco chic favoured by diplomats and the in-crowd, continuing the legacy that began with the building's first incarnation as the jazzy Alcron Hotel in 1930. Period furnishings and fittings compete for attention with mod-cons and the snappy can-do attitude of the staff. Non-smoking and disabled rooms available.
☎ 222 820 000 🖳 www.radissonsas.com ✉ Štěpánská 40, Nové Město Ⓜ Muzeum ✖ Alcron; La Rotonde ⚖

Renaissance Prague Hotel (4, G3) This Marriott hotel caters particularly well to the business traveller by offering professional service, work-ready rooms, and a business centre with photocopying, printing and a typing service. Also has a fitness centre with a pool and gym.
☎ 221 821 111
🖳 www.renaissancehotels.com ✉ V celnici 7, Nové Město Ⓜ Náměstí Republiky ✖ Seven; U Korbele ⚖

U Zlaté studně (5, C2) Commandeering one end of a narrow winding lane, this Renaissance edifice crams in a lot of antique-enhanced luxury. City vistas prompt fantasies of the 'one day all this will be yours' variety, particularly from the restaurant's glorious outdoor terrace.
☎ 257 011 213
🖳 www.zlatastudna.cz ✉ U Zlaté Studně 4, Malá Strana Ⓜ Malostranská ✖ Restaurant U Zlaté studně

Baroque Hotel Questenberk

TOP END

Ametyst (3, B3) This grand white edifice looks slightly out of place (and scale) on this very quiet backstreet in Vinohrady, but it's a friendly, if somewhat somnolent, place, with bright, squeaky-clean and attractively furnished rooms. There's a sauna, solarium and massage available for the travel-weary, and a couple of limousines to whisk you to and from the airport.
☎ 222 921 921 ▢ www.hotelametyst.cz ✉ Jana Masaryka 11, Vinohrady Ⓜ Náměstí Míru ✗ La Galleria; Vienna ♿

Domus Henrici (2, C2) This hotel is intentionally nondescript out the front, hinting that peace and privacy are the top priorities here. Stylish rooms, half of which have a desk, Internet point and fax/copier/scanner for work-occupied visitors, spill out onto terraces which have sigh-inducing views over Prague.
☎ 220 511 369 ▢ www.hidden-places.com ✉ Loretánsk 11, Hradčany Ⓜ Malostranská, then tram 22 or 23 to Pohořec ✗ U Labutí (p63) ♿

Hotel Adria (4, E5) Conveniently located in the busiest part of town, the smart Adria is popular with tour groups and business travellers, with 24hr Internet access, secretarial service and conference rooms. Bedrooms are functionally comfortable and there are a couple of on-site restaurants and bars.
☎ 221 081 111 ▢ www.adria.cz ✉ Václavské náměstí 26, Nové Město Ⓜ Můstek ✗ Triton; Café Neptun

Hotel Astoria (7, E1) This apartment-block hotel is

Guards in Hotel Kampa

pleasant, modern and in a good central position. Rooms are comfortable with a contemporary feel and staff are welcoming. Rooms on the 7th floor come with balconies.
☎ 221 775 711 ▢ www.hotelastoria.cz ✉ Rybná 10, Staré Město Ⓜ Náměstí Republiky ✗ Astoria

Hotel Elite (4, D6) Guests sleep underneath frescos or paint-daubed wooden beams in this classically refurbished house. And when the antique fittings close in on you, try hitting the refreshing atrium bar, or the cellar bar with its regular live jazz. Indulge in the full gamut of services, including secretarial, laundry and a beauty parlour, and it's only a block from the shopping on Národní třída.
☎ 224 932 250 ▢ www.hotelelite.cz ✉ Ostrovní 32, Nové Město Ⓜ Národní třída ✗ Ultramarin

Accommodation Agencies

Listed are some reputable accommodation agencies covering everything from hostels to luxury hotels and private accommodation. Some agencies prefer you pay first and then see a place, whereas you'll probably want it the other way around – if in doubt, be persistent.

AVE (☎ 224 223 226; ▢ www.avetravel.cz; ✉ offices at airport & main train station)
Happy House Rentals (☎ 222 312 488; ▢ www.happyhouserentals.com; 4, F2; ✉ Soukenická 8, Staré Město)
ESTEC (☎ 257 210 410; ▢ estec@jrc.cz)
Top Tour (☎ 224 819 111; fax 224 811 400; 7, F2; ✉ Rybná 3, Staré Město)

Hotel Kampa (4, A5) In this Best Western medieval theme park you'll find that subtlety is an unknown quantity, particularly in the feasting hall which is buried beneath candelabras and suits of armour. However, the rooms are surprisingly modern and you'll find yourself in one of the less-trammelled parts of the Small Quarter.
☎ 257 404 444
🖳 www.euroagentur.cz
✉ Všehrdova 16, Malá Strana Ⓜ Národní třída, then tram 22, 23 or 57 to jezd ✕ Knight Hall ♿

Hotel Rott (7, C3) This well-located newcomer has a fresh, clean look about it, and offers all the mod-cons you could wish for, including interactive TVs in each room for Internet access. It has a 2-storey studio for longer stays, with a kitchen and 'workroom'.
☎ 224 190 901 🖳 www .hotelrott.cz ✉ Malé náměstí 4, Staré Město Ⓜ Staroměstská ✕ Paleta; U Rotta (p75) ♿

Hotel U Brány (5, B3) Very pleasant and friendly hotel offering ten spacious, wooden-beam ceiling apartments, all with large bathrooms; the attic apartment has a splendid view of the castle. There's also a good restaurant and a well-stocked wine-bar where you can sip a vast range of wines and 35 types of whiskey. Big discounts often available.
☎ 257 531 227 🖳 www .ubrany.cz ✉ Nerudova 21, Malá Strana Ⓜ Malostranská ✕ Nerudovka

Hotel U Prince (7, C3) Accommodation-wise, you won't get closer to Old Town Square unless you camp at the feet of Jan Hus. Recently renovated, this Gothic hotel lacks the vast spaces common in other top-end places and has only six rooms per floor, giving it a personalised feel. Live jazz nightly in the restaurant.
☎ 224 213 807
🖳 www.hoteluprince.cz
✉ Staroměstské náměstí 29, Staré Město Ⓜ Staroměstská ✕ ♿

Rezidence Lundborg (4, A3) Beautifully restored 700-year-old house looking towards historic Charles Bridge, with gleaming contemporary suites, some with painted ceilings, and each with its own kitchen and free Internet access. Great family or group base.
☎ 257 011 911 🖳 www .lundborg.se ✉ U lužického semináře 3, Malá Strana Ⓜ Malostranská ✕ Blue Lion Bar ♿

Hotel U Brány in Malá Strana has an apartment for you

MID-RANGE

Aparthotel Lublaňka (3, A3) This is a friendly place offering simply decorated but clean and homey apartments, sleeping between two and six people. All have kitchen, satellite TV and phone, and breakfast is included.

☎ 222 510 041
🖥 www.lublanka.cz
✉ Lublaňska 59, Vinohrady Ⓜ IP Pavlova 🍴 Alexander Veliki (p76) ♿

Hotel Abri (3, C3) Pleasant, if somewhat anonymous, small hotel on a very quiet street, with plain but contemporary and comfortable rooms, including one well fitted out for disabled guests. There's a safe hotel parking lot and a decent restaurant offering traditional Czech food on-site.

☎ 222 515 124
🖥 abri@login.cz ✉ Jana Masaryka 36, Vinohrady Ⓜ Náměstí Míru 🍴

'Golden Cross' at night in Wenceslas Square

Hotel Antik (4, E2) As the name suggests, this place has a passion for bric-a-brac, with an antique shop on the ground floor, and various pieces scattered elsewhere throughout the place. The twelve cosy rooms have been thoroughly modernised though, and there's a very pleasant courtyard garden to take breakfast.

☎ 222 322 288
🖥 www.hotelantik.cz
✉ Dlouhá 22, Josefov Ⓜ Náměstí Republiky 🍴 Lary Fary (p65)

Hotel Bílá Labuť (4, H2) Big Best Western hotel in a quiet location not far from the city centre. From the outside the hotel resembles a '70s apartment block, but on the inside it has been thoroughly modernised with the needs of business travellers especially in mind. There's a fitness centre and sauna, a couple of restaurants, and pet-owners will be pleased to hear that pussy or pooch is welcome, free of charge.

☎ 224 811 382
🖥 cchotels@login.cz
✉ Biskupsk 9, Nové Město Ⓜ Náměstí Republiky 🍴

Hotel Esplanade (4, G5) Thoroughly opulent hotel with a certain fin-de-siècle ambience engendered by all the drapery, chandeliers, marble and Art Nouveau stylings. The more richly-decorated rooms may be a touch over-the-top for some, but there's a variety of rooms for you to choose from. Other facilities include a club bar, restaurant, meeting rooms, congress hall and a babysitting service.

☎ 224 501 111
🖥 www.esplanade.cz
✉ Washingtonova 19, Nové Město Ⓜ Hlavní Nádraží 🍴 ♿

Hotel Na Zlatém Kříži (4, E5) The hotel 'On the Golden Cross' – 'golden cross' being estate agent-speak for the seedy intersection of 28.října and Wenceslas Square – has a warm, dark wood-enhanced feel and is cheap for the city centre. There are only two (slightly musty) rooms on each floor, so make sure you book early; note there's no elevator.

☎ 224 219 501 🖥 www.goldencross.cz ✉ Jungmannovo náměstí 2, Nové Město Ⓜ Můstek 🍴 Káva Káva Káva (p69)

Hotel Sax (5, B4) Down a flight of old stairs from Nerudova is this friendly, ultra-modern hotel. Despite planting itself firmly in the present, the Hotel Sax is refreshingly low-key and unpretentious, from its tidy, uncluttered rooms and naturally lit atrium to its understated entrance marquee.

☎ 257 531 268
🖥 www.hotelsax.cz
✉ Jánský vršek 3, Malá Strana Ⓜ Malostranská 🍴 U Zeleného Čaje

Hotel Sofia (3, B3) If your tastes tend to veer towards the Spartan, then this simple Bulgarian-run hotel might be the one for you. Snoozing away in a quiet part of Vinohrady, it favours lots of dated brown furnishings in its public areas, though the rooms are rather lighter. Buffet breakfast included.

☎ 224 255 711
🖳 sofia@avetravel
✉ Americká 28, Vinohrady Ⓜ Náměstí Míru
🍴 Mehana Sofia (p76)

Hotel Ungelt (7, E2) Unique and stylish, all-suite boutique hotel conveniently positioned right in the heart of the Old Town. The oldest part of the hotel dates back to the 12th-century, and inside, it's an interesting mix of Gothic and Renaissance decor, with plenty of chandeliers and swept-back drapery. All suites have kitchens, and if you fancy a lie in, breakfast will be delivered to your room.

☎ 224 828 686
🖳 www.ungelt.cz
✉ Štupartská 1, Staré Město Ⓜ Náměstí Republiky 🍴 Rybí trh (p74)

Junior Hotel & Hostel (4, G4) Handy for the main train station, this small, recently refurbished hotel has fairly standard but perfectly acceptable rooms. There's also a much cheaper hostel on the same site and under the same management, with doubles, triples and quads. If you're lost for something to do of an evening, take yourself

Patrons enjoy the autumn sunshine in Old Town Square

downstairs to the hotel's basement for a spot of ten pin bowling.

☎ 224 231 754
🖳 www.euroagentur.cz
✉ Senovážné náměstí 21, Nové Město Ⓜ Hlavní Nádraží 🍴 Pasta e Basta

Pension Museum (4, F6) This is a very simple pension with 24hr reception, right off the hubbub of Wenceslas Square and with rooms overlooking a peaceful courtyard. Sadly, the grumpy staff tend to wear the trademark Prague scowl to greet guests.

☎ 296 325 186 ✉ Mezibranská 15, Nové Město

Ⓜ Muzeum 🍴 Taj Mahal (p71)

U Krále Jiřího (7, A4) 'King George's' is a 14th-century edifice with smallish, simple rooms, some come complete with head-bumping wooden beams. It's within lurching distance of Old Town Square although the bar is so comfortable that you may not venture outside. Unfortunately there's no lift, only some steep stairs.

☎ 222 220 925
🖳 www.kinggeorge.cz
✉ Liliová 10, Staré Město Ⓜ Staroměstská
🍴 Reykjavík (p74)

Pet-Friendly

Following are a few of the hotels and pensions around Prague that are willing to help save you the heartbreak of putting your trusty nonhuman companion into a facility where they're treated like royalty while you're away: **Hotel Savoy** (p97), **Hotel Bílá Labuť** (p100), **Hotel/Pension City** (p102), and **Unitas Pension** (p102).

BUDGET

Clown and Bard Hostel
(6, D3) One of Prague's most popular hostels, offering simple but spotless doubles, dorms (4-6 beds) and 6-bed flats with kitchens for larger groups. Attracts an international youthful crowd, most of whom end up in the lively cellar bar, which hosts regular guest DJ nights and movies.
☎ 222 716 453 🖳 www.clownandbard.com ✉ Bořivojova 102, Žižkov Ⓜ Hlavní Nádraží then tram 5, 9 or 26 🍴

Hostel Týn
(7, D1) Cheap place offering dorms and doubles in a very central location, hidden away in a courtyard just off Old Town Square. A bargain if you want to be in the heart of things, and predictably, books up quickly.
☎ 224 828 519 🖳 www.hostel-tyn.web2001.cz ✉ Týnská 19, Staré Město Ⓜ Náměstí Republiky 🍴 Beas (p72)

Pretty Kavárna Imperial

Hotel/Pension City
(3, B3) Clean, family-run pension, with simple rooms in a quiet, leafy area. The main difference between the pension and hotel rooms is a private bathroom in the former; mod cons like TV and phone cost extra. Good news for the animal kingdom — pets are welcome.
☎ 222 521 606 🖳 www.hotelcity.cz ✉ Belgická 10, Vinohrady Ⓜ Náměstí Míru 🍴 Bumerang (p76) ♿

Hotel Imperial
(4, G2) The deep, dark corridors and air of bygone intrigue hovering over the Imperial provide an atmospheric glimpse of old Prague. The very simple rooms, and the communal showers and toilets could do with a thorough overhaul, but this is still amazing value for the location. Come now before it's redeveloped by an international luxury chain.
☎ 224 816 607 🖳 reservation@hotelimperial.cz ✉ Na Poříčí 15, Nové Město Ⓜ Náměstí Republiky 🍴 Kavárna Imperial (p69)

Sir Toby's Hostel
(6, D2) This exemplary smoke-free hostel, in a newly refurbished building, has the brightest facade on the street. Helpful staff can give info on the neighbourhood and Prague in general.
☎ 283 870 635 🖳 www.sirtobys.com ✉ Dělnická 24, Holešovice Ⓜ Nádraží Holešovice

Bright Café Screen in the brooding Hotel Imperial

Travellers' Hostel
(4, F2) The only one of five Travellers' Hostels open year-round, this place offers the usual basic dorms, use of a kitchen and Internet access, though it can be a bit noisy. Another 'branch' (with huge dorms) is on Střelecký ostrov (open end of May-Sep).
☎ 224 826 662 🖳 www.travellers.cz ✉ Dlouhá 33, Staré Město Ⓜ Náměstí Republiky 🍴 Dahab Yalla (p64)

Unitas Pension
(4, C5) Every man, woman and their dog are welcome here. Those keen to sample the retro-communist vibe can eschew a private room for a bunk in a former secret police prison cell where former president Havel was once held. Basic but unforgettable.
☎ 224 221 802 🖳 www.unitas.cz ✉ Bartolomějská 9, Staré Město Ⓜ Národní třída 🍴 Konvikt Pub

About Prague

Historically rich Prague has a vivacious personality which has gone on a decade-long shopping spree and bought itself a new, hip wardrobe. Its boulevards and laneways have outstanding combinations of the classically old and the head-spinningly modern. Grandly preserved buildings on stone-floored streets host stylish bars and restaurants, while sculpture-encrusted theatres and Romanesque cellars echo with the sounds of orchestras and musos jazzing or rocking themselves into a sweat.

Not that this is any secret. Visitors have been coming to Prague for years to absorb the magnificent architectural legacies of castles and churches, and the commercial whirlwind of creative arts. Prague's rampant popularity is obvious to anyone who's been confronted with a tourist pack sweeping towards them down one of the city's narrow streets like a tsunami, leaving them clinging to an old building in its wake. But even the crowds can sometimes add something special, like when you're sitting in a small *náměstí* and suddenly it fills with a tide of people who just as quickly depart, leaving you to savour their transience and appreciate the solitude even more.

Serene Strahov Monastery on Petřín Hill

The locals can sometimes be famously indifferent, but often this is just a tourist-weary facade or an indigenous bluntness. Don't be fooled into thinking that a gruff noise is the start and end of communication – shrug your assumptions to the floor, try a few words of broken Czech, and see what happens. Not bad as a mantra for your stay in Prague, really.

HISTORY
In the Beginning

People have been setting up home in the general area around Prague since 600,000 BC, and farming communities settled here from 4000 BC. The region was then occupied by Germanic and Celtic tribes, and in the 6th century, two Slav tribes, the Czechs and the Zličani, settled on either side of the Vltava.

The Czech Přemysl dynasty established Prague Castle in the 870s. Christianity was adopted during the rule of 'Good King' Wenceslas from 925–35, and in 950 Bohemia was engulfed by the Holy Roman Empire. Under Charles IV's rule (1346–78), Prague prospered and acquired landmarks like Charles Bridge and St Vitus Cathedral.

Hussites & Hapsburgs

Jan Hus led his Christian-reform movement (Hussitism) in the late 14th and early 15th centuries. He was burned at the stake in 1415, provoking a rebellion that eventually put the Hussites in charge; their king from 1452–71 was George of Poděbrady. The Czech nobility arranged for the Austrian Catholic Hapsburgs to rule in 1526, and Prague became the Hapsburg seat. But an uprising in 1618 resulted in the Thirty Years' War, the death of a quarter of the region's population, and ultimately the loss of Czech independence for 250 years.

A Word of Hurt

Czechs are responsible for the introduction of a rather unpleasant word to the English language. The word is 'defenestration', which means 'the act of throwing a thing or especially a person out of a window'. It was coined in 1419 when Hussites, still angry about the execution of their figurehead four years earlier, threw several Catholic councillors out of an upper window of Prague's New Town Hall. The incident was reprised with devastating consequences in 1618 when a couple of Hapsburg councillors left Prague Castle in similar fashion, sparking off the Thirty Years War.

Czech National Revival

Literature, journalism, architecture and drama flourished in Prague during the 19th-century Czech National Revival. One attempt to reclaim Czech identity was historian František Palacký's seminal *Dějiny národu Českého* (History of the Czech Nation). In 1861, Czechs finally wrested control of Prague in council elections, but the country remained under Austrian rule.

Independence & War

An unwillingness to support Austrian or Hungarian WWI causes led to international pleas from Czechs and Slovaks for independence, and on 28 October 1918, Czechoslovakia was born. Its capital was Prague, which then expanded by swallowing surrounding settlements.

By 1939 German forces had occupied Bohemia and Moravia. By the time WWII concluded, the Nazis had devastated nearly all of Prague's 120,000-strong Jewish population. One of the newly reinstated government's first acts was to expel Sudeten Germans, and thousands perished in forced marches to Bavaria and Austria.

Communism

The Communist Party won over one-third of the Czechoslovakian popular vote in the 1946 elections and formed a coalition government with other socialist parties. But after intense bickering with local democrats, the communists seized control with the Soviet Union's support in 1948. The next decade and a half saw economic policies that brought Czechoslovakia close to financial ruin, and an intolerance of political rivals that led to widespread persecution, and the deaths of thousands of people by execution.

'Prague Spring' & Charter 77

In the late 1960s, national Communist Party leader Alexander Dubček showed reformist colours through rapid liberalisation under the banner of 'socialism with a human face'. The Soviet regime crushed this 'Prague Spring' on the night of 20-21 August 1968 with Warsaw-Pact military hardware. In January 1977, a document called Charta 77 (Charter 77) was signed by nearly 250 intellectuals and artists, including Václav Havel – this public demand for basic human rights became an anti-communist tenet for dissidents.

National Velvet

A violent attack by police on hundreds of people attending a rally in Prague on 17 November 1989 generated continuous public demonstrations, culminating in 750,000 people gathering on Letná plain. A group led by Havel procured the government's resignation on 3 December, and 26 days later he was the new leader. This period of nonviolent demonstration became known as the Velvet Revolution. Peaceful 'problem-solving' was repeated when Slovak and Czech leaders agreed to go their separate ways on 1 January 1993, the day Prague became capital of the new Czech Republic and Havel its president.

New Independence

Subsequent years have unfortunately been marred by financial scandals and a highly unpopular power-sharing arrangement between the two main parties. Havel barely weathered the 1998 presidential elections, scraping in by a wafer-thin margin, and stepped down in 2003 as Václav Klaus took over the reins.

Since the end of communism, Prague has seen a rise in crime and a deterioration in health and housing, though this has been partly compensated for by a strengthened economy and an increase in tourist dollars.

ENVIRONMENT

Traffic snarls are a major source of noxious irritation for anyone out for a walk in the late afternoon, particularly anywhere within breathing distance of Wenceslas Square. This, however, is nothing compared to the fume-laden haze that settles during the occasional winter inversions.

Avoid the traffic by hiring a bike

The Vltava has a less-than-pristine reputation when it comes to water quality, no thanks to industrial pollution of the past and the increasing traffic plying the water in the name of tourism. But some fearless (or brainless) people have been spotted taking morning dips off

Slovanský ostrov, and early evening on the riverbank off Josefov often finds someone with a line in the water.

Recycling is deeply imprinted on Czech domestic life, with large bins accepting paper, plastics and glassware in prominent locations. If staying in a private apartment in the Old Town, you may also be treated to a touch of noise pollution from late-night revellers or the ubiquitous municipal worker 'fixing' the paving just under your window.

Prague suffered its worst flood in centuries in August 2002, with large parts of the city underwater and the metro system inoperable for months afterwards. Some of the sorriest scenes were at the zoo, which was decimated and many animals killed. The clean-up continued until well into 2003, though Prague has since made a healthy comeback.

Changing the guard at Prague Castle

GOVERNMENT & POLITICS

Prague is the capital of the Czech Republic, a parliamentary democracy with a president (currently Václav Klaus) chosen by parliament for a five-year term. The president in turn chooses the prime minister, who along with the cabinet (*vláda*) holds the real decision-making power. The parliament has a House of Representatives (*poslanecká sněmovna*) and a Senate (*sénat*), both publicly elected.

Prague's governing body, the Local Government of the Capital City of Prague, has its seat elsewhere and is represented by a municipal office acting in concert with a mayor-headed council. The city contains 10 districts and 57 suburbs, each with their own district and local governments.

The Prague electorate has lately favoured the right-leaning Civic Democratic Party (ODS), in contrast to a national trend supporting the left-leaning Social Democrats (ČSSD), whose leader is current Prime Minister Vladimir Spidla. The Communist party still has a dedicated core (albeit an elderly one) of supporters.

The people of Prague voted overwhelmingly in favour of joining the EU in 2003, and the Czech Republic becomes a full member in 2004.

ECONOMY

The Czech Republic has been fighting back from a recession in 1998 and saw its economy grow by 2.5% in 2001. The majority of Prague's population are employed in one of the service industries, and a large proportion of those are connected in some way to the ever-growing local tourist industry. The swelling number of foreigners making the trip out to Prague contributes enormously to the local economy and obviously has a flow-on effect impacting the entire Czech Republic.

Unfortunately, many tourists are contributing too much due to the 'one price for them, one price for us' system applied by some establishments in the main tourist districts. This two-tiered pricing often results in visitors paying twice as much for their accommodation and entertainment as the local Czechs.

Roughly 10% of the population is employed in the manufacturing industry, specifically textiles, food and machinery. These activities take place mainly in the industrial suburbs of Smíchov and Karlín.

SOCIETY & CULTURE

Czechs have a west Slavic background. The two main minority groups in Prague are Romany (gypsies) and Slovaks. There are also several sizeable expat communities, mainly contingents of Americans, Germans and Ukrainians, and growing numbers of British and Irish; it's thought they make up about 4-5% of Prague's total population.

Czechs tend to be restrained socially, though they often let their hair down in the more popular beerhalls or non-tourist bars or restaurants. One of their strongest characteristics is a sense of humour, but it's hard to appreciate if you don't understand the language. Generally, the people of Prague are polite and mild-mannered – the few exceptions include life-or-death football fans, staff in some upmarket tourist places, and everybody who shops in the supermarket at Tesco. On a serious note, though admittedly rare, there have occasionally been reports of muggings, and attacks by skinheads on dark-skinned people.

> **Did you Know?**
> - Population 1.2 million
> - Inflation 3.8%
> - Unemployment less than 3%
> - Average Czech monthly wage 15,700Kč
> - Average price of pub beer 20Kč/ 500mL

Roma (Gypsies)

Roma or gypsies (*romové* or *cikáni*) are a minority group (0.3%) with a lineage that extends back to 15th-century India. They suffer neglect and hostility across the Czech Republic and Central Europe, due to a lack of acceptance of their generally closed, transient lifestyle; Roma involvement in petty theft and fraud in lieu of the unskilled work they are normally restricted to; and, unfortunately, to flat-out racism.

The lack of Czech action to address the Roma's disproportionate levels of poverty, illiteracy and unemployment has been criticised by the EU.

Some common Czech civilities, which are also appreciated when uttered by visitors, include the following phrases: *dobrý den* (good morning); *dobrý večer* (good evening); *prosím* (please); *na shledanou* (goodbye) and *nazdravi* (cheers).

Etiquette

When attending most shows around town, you can rock up wearing pretty much anything you want (though couples wearing matching slacks and jackets should note such outfits violate international fashion laws). If you're going to the opera, ballet or a concert at the larger or more traditional venues, however, smart casual is the preferred style; outside upmarket private functions black tie will look out of place, as will the tourist uniform of baseball cap and shorts.

Smoking is common and there are few places that restrict or ban the activity, with obvious exceptions being inside public transport, museums, galleries and the like. It's the custom in many eateries to resist smoking over lunch, even if there are ashtrays on the table – if in doubt, ask a waiter.

ARTS
Architecture

The earliest architectural style you'll encounter in Prague is Romanesque (10th-12th centuries), featuring heavy stone walls with small windows; fine examples include the Basilica of St George and the Old Town Hall cellar.

Gothic architecture (13th-16th centuries), built around ribbed vaults with high pointed arches, is exemplified by St Vitus' facade and the spindly heights of Týn Church. Renaissance architecture (15th-17th centuries) is classical, symmetrical, and often decorated with *sgraffito* (a multilayered mural technique), as at Schwarzenberg Palace on Hradcanské náměstí. The aggressively gaudy baroque approach (17th-18th centuries) is on display in St Nicholas Church in Malá Strana, and (unbelievably) it led to an even more over-the-top style called rococo; see the fancy dress costume worn by Kinský Palace.

Gothic architecture, St Vitus Cathedral

The revivalist period (late 18th-19th centuries) made the city like old, with resurrected styles applied to buildings like the neo-Renaissance National Theatre, while colourful Art Nouveau (circa 1899–1912) produced the exotic splendour of Municipal House. Also in the early 20th century, cubism appeared in structures like the House of the Black Madonna, after which Art Deco, plain old functionalism and fantastically ugly communist residential blocks found their place in the city. The mixed styles post-1989 are hard to quantify but can be brilliantly original, such as in the form of the Dancing Building.

Painting

The Czech Republic has a roll-call of prominent artists stretching back at least 600 years. Magister Theodoricus' painting impressed other Central European artists in the 14th century and can be seen in St Vitus' Chapel of St Wenceslas. Realism was a hit in the 19th century, with Mikuláš Aleš and the Mánes family leading the charge – and Josef was heavily influenced by romanticism.

Art Nouveau's patron saint was Alfons Mucha, whose back-catalogue is at the Mucha Museum. Famous impressionists of the same period included Max Švabinský and Antonín Slaviček. In the 20th century, an assortment

Popular Art Nouveau by Alfons Mucha

of avant-garde and cubist artists like Josef Čapek, and symbolists like František Kupka made way for the surrealism of František Janoušek and later the socialist realism of Joseph Brož. The last few decades have seen artists making grotesquery brush strokes (Jiří Načeradský) and fusing with electronic media (Woody Vašulka). The work of most of these artists is displayed at the Centre For Modern & Contemporary Art in Holešovice.

Literature

František Palacký's voluminous history of Bohemia and Moravia, the poems of Karel Hynek Mácha, and the romanticism of Božena Němcová were some of Czech literature's 19th-century stand-outs. Czech writers have a habit of becoming presidents: author and philosopher Tomáš Masaryk was Czechoslovakia's first leader, while former President Havel is a well-known scribe of plays and political commentary.

Cottage Kafka

Kafka may not have anticipated or much less desired it, but the man is a growth industry in Prague. Various venues either advertise a personal connection or invent an association. Places that were personally occupied by Kafka's stylised paranoia include his birthplace on the edge of Old Town Square (7, C1); Dum U minuty (7, C3), where he lived from 1889–96; the Little Blue Cottage (8, E1) in Golden Lane where he lived from 1916–17; and the venerable insurance office where he worked from 1908–22 (4, G3). Places that weren't, but wish they had been, include the Franz Kafka Café (7, B1), and an eponymous bookshop and a gallery (7, C2), both on Old Town Square.

Little Blue Cottage, Golden Lane

At the start of the 20th century, Franz Kafka wrote about his worst fears in *The Castle*, while Max Brod wrote about Kafka. Karel Čapek gave science fiction the robot treatment in *RUR* (Rossum's Universal Robots), and poet Jaroslav Seiffert's efforts pre-WWII eventually led to the Nobel Prize for Literature in 1984. Milan Kundera's books are well known internationally, as is the work of Ivan Klima who wrote *The Ship Named Hope* and an excellent collection of essays, *The Spirit of Prague*. Bohumil Hrabal's *The Little Town That Stood Still* is another international hit.

Music

Traditional folk music prevailed in Bohemia and Moravia until after 950, when the Church tried to impose a Gregorian alternative. In the mid-19th century a crop of great composers emerged, among them Bedřich Smetana (1824–84), an advocate of the National Revival, and Antonín Dvořák (1841–1904), who produced fine chamber music and symphonies. Other notables were Leoš Janáček (1854–1928) and Jaroslav Ježek (1882–1969).

Prague has a deep-rooted jazz scene, with Czechs figuring prominently in European jazz circles until the 1948 communist coup d'état. The 1960s brought a less-censorial atmosphere and the appearance of Prague's first professional jazz club, Reduta (see p86). Names familiar to local aficionados include Jiřví Stivín and Milan Viklický. Czechs are no slouches on the rock/pop scene either, with a number of good (though often underground) bands pre-1989,

Composer, Antonín Dvořák

and since then everything from hard rock and country & western to Roma classicists and obligatory pop specialists like Lucie Bílá.

Directory

Astronomical Clock

ARRIVAL & DEPARTURE

Air

Praha Ruzyně airport (6, A2) is about 20km west of the city centre, accessible by a combination of bus and metro. The main building shelters an arrival hall and a departure hall. Facilities include a bar, fast-food outlets, Internet access, several travel and accommodation agencies, and a scattering of ATMs and money exchange offices.

Information

General Inquiries	☎ 220 113 314
Car Park Information	☎ 220 113 408

Hotel Booking Service
Čedok	☎ 220 113 744
AVE	☎ 220 114 650

Flight Information
ČSA	☎ 220 104 111
Air France	☎ 221 662 662
British Airways	☎ 222 114 444
KLM	☎ 233 090 933
Lufthansa	☎ 220 114 456

AIRPORT ACCESS

Public transport information is available from Ruzyně airport office in the city transport department (Dopravní podnik, or DP; ☎ 220 115 404; www.dp-praha.cz).

Bus & Metro From in front of the airport's main building, catch bus No 119 or No 254 to Dejvická metro station, then ride line A into the centre; the trip takes about 45 minutes. Alternatively, bus Nos 179 and 225 run to Nové Butovice metro station in Prague's southwest, from where line B heads into town.

Bus & Tram Between midnight and 3.30am, catch night bus No 510 and transfer to city-bound tram No 51 at Divoká Šárka stop.

Taxi There's a desk in the Arrivals Hall for Airport Cars (☎ 220 113 892; ◷ 8am-11pm); no other taxis can stop outside the Arrivals Hall. A trip into the city will cost upwards of 600Kč per person, depending on the destination. From Old Town Square in a regular taxi, you'll pay around 450-500Kč to the airport.

Minibus Vans operated by Cedaz (☎ 220 114 296) run between the airport and náměstí Republiky for 90Kč per person. The vehicles can also be commissioned to drive from the airport to anywhere in the centre for 360Kč for up to four people (720Kč five-eight people). Cedaz operates from the airport from 6am-9pm, and from náměstí Republiky 5.30am-9.30pm.

Bus

The state bus company, Czech Automobile Transport (ČSAD), operates regional and long-distance domestic coaches from Florenc bus station (4, J3). Information is available in Florenc's central hall at window No 8 (◷ 6am-9pm), online (www.jizdnirady.cz), or by premium-rate phone (☎ 900 149 044; 14Kč per minute).

A number of international coaches service Prague, including a Czech line handled by Bohemia Euroexpress International (4, J2; ☎ 224 814 450; ▯ www.bei.cz; Křižikova 4-6) near Florenc bus station, and those belonging to the Eurolines consortium, whose main Prague agent is Sodeli CZ (4, G4; ☎ 224 239 318; Senovážné náměstí 6). Most coaches operate from stands at Florenc bus station and from one at Nádraží Holešovice metro station.

Train

Inexpensive and reliable domestic services are provided by Czech

Railways (ČD). You can buy plain tickets *(jízdenka)* or tickets with a reservation *(místenka)* for a seat, couchette or sleeper; when scanning timetables, look out for services designated 'R' (reservations recommended) or a circled/boxed 'R' (reservations mandatory).

Most international trains pull up at the multilevel main train station, Praha Hlavní Nádraží (4, H5; ☎ 224 615 786), though some end up at stations at Smíchov (6, B4) and Holešovice (4, C2). For information on rail connections, call ☎ 221 111 122 or visit the website www.cd.cz.

Travel Documents
PASSPORT
Those requiring a visa to visit the Czech Republic must have a passport valid for at least three months longer than the validity of the visa.

VISA
Nationals of the United Kingdom can stay in the Czech Republic for 180 days without a visa, while citizens of other EU countries plus New Zealand and the USA can visit visa-free for 90 days. Australians and Canadians have to apply to a Czech embassy or consulate for a tourist visa (visas are no longer issued at the airport or border crossings): Australians are charged a fixed rate of A$73 for 90-day single/multiple entry visas, while Canadians pay CAD$74/148.

RETURN/ONWARD TICKET
A return or onward ticket is usually (but for some reason not always) required to gain entry to the Czech Republic.

Customs & Duty Free
Visitors can import or export unlimited amounts of foreign currency, and up to 350,000Kč in Czech currency.

You can import 2L of wine, 1L of spirits and 200 cigarettes without paying duty, as well as gifts (non-commercial goods) collectively worth under 6000Kč; quantities of these goods over the specified limits have to be declared on arrival. Treat that potential antique buy of a lifetime with caution, as the real deal cannot be exported. And when on a shopping spree, remember that purchases exceeding 30,000Kč attract a 22% duty.

Left Luggage
There is a 24 hour left-luggage service in the Arrival Hall that charges 40Kč per piece of luggage.

GETTING AROUND

Prague's cheap, extensive and relatively easy public transport system is run by its transport department (Dopravní podnik; www.dp-praha .cz), which maintains information centres at the airport and in five metro stations, including Muzeum (4, G6; ☎ 222 623 777; ☺ 7am-9pm) and Můstek (4, F5; ☎ 222 646 350; ☺ 7am-6pm). Most visitors rely on the underground metro to sweep them from one side of the city to the other. Trams are also convenient, with 26 daytime routes and a handful of night-time services negotiating all the main inner city areas. Buses are mostly useful for filling in the urban gaps in the metro and tram systems, as they cover pretty much everywhere beyond the centre. Pick up the detailed *Prague Transport* pamphlet from an information office.

Single transfer tickets (12/6Kč) are good for all public transport for one hour from the moment you punch them into a validation machine (for 1½ hours 8pm-5am Mon-Fri and all day Sat-Sun). Single non-transfer tickets (8/4Kč) are for short hops lasting no more than 15 minutes on buses and trams, or up to four metro stations; they are not valid for the funicular or for night transport. Tickets can be bought from ticket machines in the metro stations and at newsstands, various hotels and travel agencies.

Travel Passes

Most short-stay visitors will find it cost effective to buy tickets as they need them. If you anticipate jumping on/off public transport more than half a dozen times a day over an extended period, you should buy a short-term season pass allowing unlimited use of the metro, trams, buses and the Petřín funicular for 1/3/7/15 days at a cost of 70/200/250/280Kč. Long-term season passes give you 1/3/12 months of transport time for 420/1150/3800Kč, with a 50% student discount available for the monthly and quarterly tickets. Don't forget to validate these passes the first time you use them.

Car

On a short trip to Prague, you're unlikely to need your own wheels, and the narrow, cobblestoned streets of the historic district and the newer roads choked with trams, cars and human traffic don't make driving a pleasure. If you do need to drive, however, there are a number of rental agencies with offices at the airport, including:

Avis (☎ 235 362 420; www.avis.cz; around 4100Kč/day; airport pick-up surcharge included in daily rental)

Budget (☎ 220 113 253; www .budget.cz; from around 1571Kč/day)

Czechocar CS (☎ 220 113 454; www.czechocar.cz; from 1600Kč/day)

Hertz (☎ 233 326 714; www .hertz.cz; from 2160Kč/day)

Metro

The swift, 49-station metro operates from 5am-midnight and comprises three lines, each identified by both a letter and a colour: A (green), B (yellow) and C (red). To leave a station, head for a sign saying *výstup* (exit); for a connecting line, look for a *přestup*. Disabled travellers should note that barrier-free access to platforms is more a feature of suburban metro stations than inner city ones, the exceptions being Muzeum, Vyšehrad and Hlavní Nádraží.

Tram & Bus

The numbers allocated to tram lines have one-two digits, while bus route numbers have three digits. During the 'day', trams and buses run from 4.30am-12.15am, with more limited but still fairly regular 'night' services in the intervening time; night-time routes are serviced by buses numbered 501-512. The info centres in Muzeum, Můstek, Anděl, Černý Most and Nádraží Holešovice metro stations supply timetables and route maps for the tram and bus systems.

Taxi

Unfortunately Prague has an oversupply of crooked taxi drivers who do a major disservice to the honest ones. It is illegal for taxis to stop for fares anywhere other than a designated rank, so don't flag down a cab, or use a taxi-stand in any of the main tourist areas, unless you want to be grossly overcharged. It's far better to call one of the following, usually reliable, 24 hour radio-taxis: AAA Radio Taxi (☎ 140 14); Halo Taxi (☎ 244 114 411); City Taxi (☎ 233 103 310); or Profi Taxi (☎ 261 314 151).

PRACTICALITIES

Climate & When to Go

Prague is popular year-round, but tourists are especially numerous from May to June and over Easter, Christmas and New Year's, when getting across Charles Bridge becomes impossible without a catapult. May and September, the months on either side of the hot, downpour-prone summer, usually have the best weather for exploring the city. Though the snowy winters get very cold and are susceptible to smog alerts, it can be a beautiful time to visit and accommodation is plentiful. From the beginning of the low season in October, many attractions and businesses start limiting their hours, or close until the following summer.

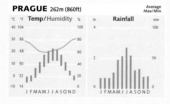

Disabled Travellers

Prague is making an effort to address the needs of disabled travellers, though facilities in some areas are still sorely lacking. Wheelchair-accessible public transport is limited to several train and metro stations with self-operating lifts, plus special buses plying two routes on weekdays linking destinations such as Hradčanská, Florenc and Náměstí Republiky; there are also two dozen mainly suburban lines serviced by low-platform buses. Pedestrian-crossing lights in the centre make a ticking noise to indicate a green light to the visually impaired, and some museums now have tactile displays and Braille text. More performance venues are being equipped with wheelchair access and some have good facilities for the hearing impaired. The 'limited', 'good' and 'excellent' disabled access ratings given to tourist sites in this book reflect the relative ease with which those in wheelchairs can reasonably visit these places. Many museums and galleries have ramps and/or lifts, enabling access to at least some of their collections. Older structures, of course, are prohibited in some cases from making such alterations to their structural fabric. Cobblestone roads may also prove difficult.

INFORMATION & ORGANISATIONS

A comprehensive source of information for wheelchair-bound travellers is the Prague Wheelchair Users Organisation (4, E2; Pražská organizace vozíčkářů; ☎ 224 827 210; www.pov.cz; Benediktská 6, Josefov). It produces the booklet *Barrier-Free Prague*, listing accessible venues, reserved parking places, transport options and tours of historical areas. The Czech-language monthly *Přehled* also lists wheelchair-friendly venues.

The Union of the Blind and Weak Sighted (4, F6; Sjednocená organizace nevidomých a slabozrakých v Čr; ☎ 221 462 146; Krakovská 21) can provide information to the vision-impaired. The website www.braillnet.cz has useful links, but only in Czech.

Discounts

Students, children under 15 and families get discounts at most tourist attractions and on public transport. Some venues offer reductions, but many just have different levels of fixed-price seating. Seniors need to be Czech citizens to qualify for local concession cards; the same applies to disabled travellers. That said, a number of places will grant concessions regardless of the formalities, and others will only have a cursory glance at the card you're waving at them.

The Prague Card offers three days of unlimited public transport and access to many museums and galleries. It's available from American Express (7, C2; Staroměstské náměstí), Čedok (7, F3; Na Příkopě 18), and several other travel agencies, and costs 560/460Kč.

YOUTH CARDS
Bring an international student identity card (ISIC). Youth cards like Euro26 and Go25 will also get you discounts at many museums, theatres and galleries, plus some hotels.

Electricity
Voltage 220V
Frequency 50 Hz
Cycle AC
Plugs two round pins

Embassies & Consulates
Australia (4, F2; ☎ 296 578 350; Unit 6/3, Solitaire Office Building, Klimentská 10, Praha 1)
Canada (6, B2; ☎ 272 101 800; Muchova 6, Praha 6)
France (4, A4; ☎ 251 171 711; Velkopřerovské náměstí 2, Malá Strana)
Germany (5, A4; ☎ 257 531 481; Vlašská 19, Praha 1)
Ireland (5, C4; ☎ 257 530 061; Tržiště 13, Malá Strana)
New Zealand (6, D4; ☎ 222 514 672; Dykova 19, Praha 1)
South Africa (6, D4; ☎ 267 311 114; Ruská 65, Praha)
UK (5, C3; ☎ 257 402 111; Thunovská 14, Praha 1)
USA (5, B4; ☎ 257 530 663; Tržiště 15, Praha 1)

Emergencies
Ambulance	☎ 155
Fire	☎ 150
Police (municipal)	☎ 156
Police (national)	☎ 158
Rape Crisis Line	☎ 257 317 100

Fitness
GYMS
Fitness Club Inter-Continental (4, D2; ☎ 296 631 525; www.prague.intercon tinental.com; náměstí Curieových 43/5, Josefov) The usual treadmills and weights, and there's also a heated pool, golf simulator and personal trainers on hand. You can round it all off with a Thai massage.
YMCA Sport Centrum (4, G3; ☎ 224 875 811; www.scymca.cz; Na poříčí 12, Nové Město) Well-equipped exercise centre with a pool, gym and solarium.

SQUASH
ASB Squashcentrum (4, F5; ☎ 224 232 752; Václavské náměstí 15, Nové Město) This squash centre has a couple of decent courts, a ping-pong table, as well as a solarium.

TENNIS
Ostrov Štvanice (6, C2; ☎ 222 234 601; www.cltk.cz; Ostrov Štvanice, Prague Islands) This island north of Florenc metro hosts the prestigious Štvanice tennis club and a popular ice-skating rink.

Gay & Lesbian Travellers
Homosexuality is legal in the Czech Republic and the age of consent is 15. The gay scene in Prague is thriving, with a number of clubs, bars, restaurants and hotels catering to the community, and a couple of gay lifestyle magazines are available on newsstands in the city centre. It's a discreet scene, however, with the various venues scattered across town and little in the way of mainstream events to draw attention

to gay life. Several establishments tailor themselves to both gays and lesbians, but the majority are gay-oriented; only one place (A-Club; see p93) reserves evenings for lesbians. Visiting gay couples may trigger uncomfortable reactions from some locals if they display affection in public, as it remains an unfamiliar sight to many Czechs.

INFORMATION & ORGANISATIONS

Information on gay and lesbian happenings and resources is on-line at GayGuide.net Prague (www.gayguide.net/Europe/Czech/Prague). *Amigo* (www.amigo.cz) is a bi-monthly gay publication with venue/event information and lots of classifieds, while two irregularly published Czech-language lesbian magazines are *Promluv* and *Alia*.

Health
IMMUNISATIONS

It's not necessary to get any vaccinations prior to your trip to the Czech Republic.

PRECAUTIONS

Prague enjoys a good standard of public hygiene, though you may not think so if you taste the unpleasantly chlorinated but nonetheless usually drinkable tap water. A less innocuous health risk is posed by the exhaust emissions that can cloud the city in winter during periods of extremely stable weather (known in meteorological terms as inversions).

Like anywhere else, practise the usual precautions when it comes to sex; condoms are available at any of the many pharmacies (*lekárna*). See the following Pharmacies section for some 24 hour places.

INSURANCE & MEDICAL TREATMENT

Travel insurance is advisable to cover medical treatment you may need while in Prague. First-aid outside a hospital (*nemocnice*) and emergency treatment are provided free to visitors, but unless you are a EU citizen covered under a reciprocal health-care arrangement, you will have to pay full price for treatment. The cost of prescriptions is borne by all foreigners.

MEDICAL SERVICES

Hospitals and clinics with 24 hour emergency departments include:
Na Homolce (6, A4; ☎ 257 271 111; www.homolka.cz; Roentgenova 2, Motol, Praha 5)
Policlinic at Národní (4, C5; ☎ 222 075 120, 606 461 628; Národní 9, Staré Město, Praha 1)
Health Centre Prague (4, E6; ☎ 224 220 040, after hours 603 433 833; 603 481 361; No 3, 2nd fl, Vodičkova 28, Nové Město, Praha 1)

DENTAL SERVICES

For emergency treatment, head to the 24 hour Praha 1 clinic (4, E5; ☎ 224 946 986; Palackého 5, Nové Město).

PHARMACIES

The following pharmacies are open 24 hours:
Lékárna Palackého Praha 1 clinic (4, E5; ☎ 224 946 981; Palackého 5, Nové Město, Praha 1)
Lékárna U sv Ludmily (3, A2; ☎ 222 519 731; Belgická 37, Vinohrady, Praha 2)

Holidays

1 January	New Year's Day
March/April	Easter Monday
1 May	Labour Day
8 May	Liberation Day
5 July	SS Cyril & Methodius Day
6 July	Jan Hus Day
28 September	Czech Statehood Day
28 October	Independence Day
17 November	Struggle for Freedom & Democracy Day

24 December	'Generous Day', Christmas Eve
25 December	Christmas Day
26 December	St Stephen's Day

Internet

The Internet cafe scene is growing in Prague – very useful if your accommodation is not connected. However, nearly all top-end hotels have on-site facilities or data points in rooms. Internet-cafe connection speeds and charges can vary significantly, with the terminal-heavy places usually charging the lowest prices; some also have data points for plugging in your laptop.

INTERNET SERVICE PROVIDERS (ISPS)

Major ISPs you can access in Prague include AOL (www.aol.com), CompuServe (www.compuserve.com) and AT&T (www.attbusiness.net). If you have an account with one of these, you can download a list of local dial-in numbers.

INTERNET CAFES

Bohemia Bagel (7, D1; ☎ 224 812 560; www.bohemiabagel.cz; Masna 2) Second branch at Újezd 2 (5, C3).
Palác Knih Neo Luxor (4, F5; ☎ 221 111 336; Václavské náměstí 41)
Zlatá Spika (4, G3; ☎ 222 310 184; http://zlata.spika.cz; Zlatnická 11)

USEFUL WEBITES

The Lonely Planet website (www.lonelyplanet.com) is an excellent resource and offers a speedy link to many of Prague's best websites. Others to try include:
Czech Tourist Authority (www.czechtourism.cz)
Prague Castle (www.hrad.cz)
Prague Contact (www.praguecontact.com)
Prague Experience (www.pragueexperience.com)
Prague Post (www.praguepost.com)
Square Meal (www.squaremeal.cz)
Theatre Institute Prague (www.theatre.cz)

Lost Property

Try the city's lost and found office (4, C5; ztráty a nálezy; ☎ 224 235 085; Karoliny Světlé 5). Ruzyně airport has a 24 hour lost and found office (☎ 220 114 283).

Metric System

The metric system is used. Czechs use commas rather than decimal points, and points for thousands. Prices rounded to the nearest koruna are followed by a dash. See the conversion table following.

TEMPERATURE

$$°C = (°F - 32) ÷ 1.8$$
$$°F = (°C × 1.8) + 32$$

DISTANCE
1in = 2.54cm
1cm = 0.39in
1m = 3.3ft = 1.1yd
1ft = 0.3m
1km = 0.62 miles
1 mile = 1.6km

WEIGHT
1kg = 2.2lb
1lb = 0.45kg
1g = 0.04oz
1oz = 28g

VOLUME
1L = 0.26 US gallons
1 US gallon = 3.8L
1L = 0.22 imperial gallons
1 imperial gallon = 4.55L

Money
CURRENCY

The Czech currency is the *koruna* (crown), contracted from *koruna česka* to Kč. Each koruna is divided into 100 *haléřů* or heller (h). Coins come in 10 haléřů, 20 haléřů, 50 haléřů, 1Kč, 2Kč, 5Kč, 10Kč and 20Kč pieces. Notes come in denominations of 50Kč, 100Kč, 200Kč, 500Kč, 1000Kč, 2000Kč and 5000Kč. 50Kč coins and 20Kč notes exist (allegedly) but are rather scarce.

TRAVELLERS CHEQUES
Most mainstream tourist places accept travellers cheques from American Express (7, C2; ☎ 222 800 111) and Thomas Cook (4, D5; ☎ 221 105 371), but smaller businesses may refuse them.

ATMS
There's no shortage of ATMs around Prague, particularly in the areas where plastic-happy people congregate, like Na Příkopě, Wenceslas Square, náměstí Republiky, the main train station and the airport. All ATMs will process cards belonging to, or affiliated with, Maestro, MasterCard, Visa, Plus and Cirrus.

CHANGING MONEY
The best place to change money is at one of the big banks, where commissions hover around 2%. The worst place is at one of the myriad private bureaux *(směnárna)* around Wenceslas Square and throughout the Old Town. Many of these advertise zero commission, which sounds terrific until you find out this percentage applies only to the selling of currency (ie, selling you foreign currency in exchange for your koruna). When you are buying local currency, the commission they charge can be as high as 10%. Try and avoid 5000Kč and 2000Kč notes, as these can be difficult to change.

Banks are generally open 8am-5pm Monday to Friday, but counters are sometimes temporarily unattended around lunchtime.

Newspapers & Magazines
The main Czech-language daily newspapers include *Mladá fronta Dnes* and the conservative *Lidové noviny*, while the prime English-language newspaper is the slim, review-packed weekly *The Prague Post*. There's also a German-language equivalent, the *Praguer Zeitung*. The free quarterly, *Prague*, has thoughtful articles of cultural, social and business interest, plus interviews with prominent locals and visitors. It's usually available at tourist information centres. The gay magazine *Amigo* is widely available at newsstands in the centre, as are many major international newspapers and magazines.

Opening Hours
The following hours are just a rough guide, and can fluctuate wildly according to the type of business, season and location; note that tourist-oriented places are generally open longer hours and often on Sunday.

Shops 9am-6pm Mon-Fri, 10am-1pm Sat
Offices 9am-5pm Mon-Fri
Post offices 8am-6pm Mon-Fri, 8am-noon Sat
Restaurants 11am-11pm
Attractions 10am-6pm; many museums and galleries close Mon

Photography & Video
Film-processing places are in abundance, particularly in the Old Town and Malá Strana; there are a couple of decent shops in the Kotva (7, F1) and Krone (4, F5) department stores. Entrust your slides to Fotographia Praha (4, E6) or to Fototechnika (4, F5); both use a reliable lab and are located in Lucerna Passage. Fototechnika is dependable place for camera repairs.

The Czech Republic uses the PAL video system, which is incompatible with the SECAM (France) or NTSC (Japan and North America) systems. Make sure you double-check which system your own equipment is based on.

Post
Prague's postal service is fairly reliable, but for important items it's best to use registered mail *(do*

poručený dopis) or Express Mail Service (EMS). The main post office (4, F4; ☎ 221 131 445; Jindřišská 14) has an automated queuing system. Dispensers in the entrance hall issue tickets; there are instructions in English on the machines, and an information desk inside the main hall to the left. Stamps can be bought at any newsstand.

POSTAL RATES
Standard mail to domestic destinations costs 6.40Kč. Postcards/letters to elsewhere in Europe cost 9Kč, and to Australia, USA and Canada 14Kč.

Radio
Local FM radio stations specialise in country (Country Radio; 89.5), classical (Classic; 98.7), disco (Zlatá Praha; 97.2), pop (Bonton; 99.7), and hip alternative music for the masses (Radio 1; 91.9). The state-owned broadcaster is Czech Radio; its news bulletins are available daily at the Radio Prague website (www.radio.cz).

For English-language news and culture, simply switch over to the BBC World Service (101.1), which re-broadcasts in Czech, Slovak and English. There's also Radio Free Europe (1233, 1287AM).

Safety Concerns
Pickpocketing is a problem in places where tourists congregate. Visitors have also been targeted by men posing as police – one version of this scam involves the 'cops' asking to see the foreigner's money and then returning it minus a few notes (or just bolting off with the lot). The police do not have the power to search you in this manner, and if you doubt the authenticity of an official who approaches you, hang on to your wallet and passport and insist on going with them to the nearest police station. To make a police report regarding

stolen property, head to the interpreter-equipped Praha 1 police station at Jungmannovo náměstí 9 (4, E4; ☎ 261 451 760).

Prague is safe to walk around at night if you apply common sense and stay aware of your surroundings. Prostitutes, usually exploited by organised crime gangs, target tourists in the Old Town after dark. At night, avoid the park in front of the main train station.

Telephone
All Prague telephone numbers were changed in September 2002 as the modern digital system was installed, usually with an extra '2' added to the front of the old number. You must dial the full nine digits even if calling from within the city. Using payphones for local calls at peak times (7am-7pm Mon-Fri) costs around 4Kč for two minutes; rates fall by around 50% outside peak times. Note that blue phones only take coins (2-20Kč) but there are plenty of public phones that use phonecards *(telekart)* suitable for local, domestic and international calls.

Phonecards (150, 200 and 300Kč) are available from the PIS, post offices and newsagents.

MOBILE PHONES
The mobile phone network is GSM 900, which is compatible with other European and Australian phones but not with Japanese or North American models (though GSM 1800 and PCS 1900 mobiles should work). Note that since 2002, mobile numbers have dropped the initial '0'.

Television
There are two government-run television channels, ČT1 and ČT2, the latter broadcasting the English-language 'Euronews' at either noon or 1pm. There are also two private channels – Nova and Prima – that

show trashy sitcoms and soaps. Most hotels and rented apartments have satellite receivers.

Time

Czechs use the 24 hour clock. Prague Standard Time is one hour ahead of GMT/UTC. Daylight-savings time is from the last weekend in March to the last weekend of October.

Tipping

Some restaurants indicate on their menus or on your itemised bill that the final amount includes a tip; check to make sure you don't tip twice. If by some chance you feel service warrants a gratuity, tip 10-15% extra.

Toilets

Public toilets (*vé cé* or *toalet*) for men (*muži* or *páni*) and women (*ženy* or *dámy*) located in metro, train and bus stations will normally be staffed by attendants whose wages are paid by the 2-3Kč you give them for use of the facilities.

Tourist Information

The city-run Prague Information Service (Pražská informační služba, or PIS; ☎ 124 44; www.prague-info.cz) has four offices with information on the city; pick up the quarterly *Welcome to Prague* (27Kč) plus the free *Prague This Month*. Branches are at Old Town Hall (7, C2), Na Příkopě 20 (7, F3), the main train station (4, H5), and Malá Strana Bridge Tower at Mostecká 2 (4, A3; closed Nov-Mar).

The private Prague Tourist Centre (7, D4; ☎ 224 212 209; www.ptc.cz; Rytířská 12) sells guidebooks, maps and tickets to concerts and theatre around town.

Women Travellers

Prague is a safe city for women in direct comparison to other large European cities, but there has been a rise in the incidence of sexual violence towards women in the past decade, and verbal harassment is not uncommon.

Women, particularly solo travelllers, may find many neighbourhood pubs less enjoyable because of their complete domination by macho types. Don't worry there are still plenty of relaxed *vinárny* (wine bars) and alcohol-serving *kavárny* (coffee shops) to discover.

LANGUAGE

Czech (*čeština*) is obviously the main language spoken in the Czech Republic. English is widespread in central Prague but not commonly spoken in the outer suburbs and the countryside – 'widespread' doesn't mean 'always', however, and you'll often encounter people in the tourist industry who speak very little or no English. Many older citizens also speak German.

Originating from a west Slavonic linguistic grouping, Czech can be a mouthful for first-time speakers, particularly the words that are vowel-free zones. However, it doesn't take that long to begin getting the hang of some of the more common words and phrases, and the effort is often appreciated by locals. For a more detailed look at the language, get a copy of Lonely Planet's *Czech Phrasebook*.

Useful Words & Phrases

Good day.	*Dobrý den.*
Goodbye.	*Na shledanou.*
Hello/Goodbye.	*Ahoj/Čau.*
How are you?	*Jak se máte?*
Fine, thanks.	*Děkuji, dobře.*
Yes.	*Ano/Jo.*
No.	*Ne.*
Excuse me.	*S dovolením.*
Sorry.	*Promiňte.*
Please.	*Prosím.*

Thank you very much.	*Mockrát děkuji.*
That's fine/ You're welcome.	*Není zač.*
Do you speak English?	*Mluvíte anglicky?*
I don't understand.	*Nerozumím.*

Getting Around

What time does... leave/arrive?	*V kolik hodin odjíždí/přijíždí...?*
the train	*vlak*
the bus	*autobus*
Which platform?	*Které nástupiště?*
Excuse me, where is...?	*Prosím, kde je...?*
I'm looking for...	*Hledám...*
(the) ticket office	*pokladna*
I want to go to...	*Chci jet do...*
Go straight ahead.	*Jděte přímo.*
Turn left.	*Zatočte vlevo.*
Turn right.	*Zatočte vpravo.*

Buying Tickets

I'd like...	*Rád (m) bych... Ráda (f) bych...*
a one-way ticket	*jednosměrnou jízdenku*
a return ticket	*zpáteční jízdenku*
two tickets	*dvě jízdenky*

Accommodation

Do you have any rooms available?	*Máte volné pokoje?*
I'd like...	*Přál (m) bych si... Přála (f) bych si...*
a single room	*jednolůžkový pokoj*
a double room	*dvoulůžkový pokoj*
How much is it per night?	*Kolik stojí jedna noc?*

Around Town

bank	*banka*
embassy	*velvyslanectví*
information centre	*informační centrum*
main square	*hlavní náměstí*
market	*tržiště/trh*
theatre	*divadlo*
train station	*ČD/železniční nádraží*

Time & Dates

What time is it?	*Kolik je hodin?*
When?	*Kdy?*
in the morning	*ráno*
in the afternoon	*odpoledne*
in the evening	*večer*
today	*dnes*
now	*teď*

Monday	*pondělí*
Tuesday	*úterý*
Wednesday	*středa*
Thursday	*čtvrtek*
Friday	*pátek*
Saturday	*sobota*
Sunday	*neděle*

January	*leden*
February	*únor*
March	*březen*
April	*duben*
May	*květen*
June	*červen*
July	*červenec*
August	*srpen*
September	*září*
October	*říjen*
November	*listopad*
December	*prosinec*

Numbers

0	*nula*	7	*sedm*
1	*jeden*	8	*osm*
2	*dva*	9	*devět*
3	*tři*	10	*deset*
4	*čtyři*	50	*padesát*
5	*pět*	100	*sto*
6	*šest*	1000	*tisíc*

Emergencies

Help!	*Pomoc!*
I'm ill.	*Jsem nemocný/ nemocná. (m/f)*
Please call a doctor.	*Prosím, zavolejte doktora.*
ambulance	*sanitku*
police	*policii*
Where is the toilet?	*Kde je záchod?*
I'm lost.	*Zabloudil /a jsem. (m/f)*
Could you help me please?	*Prosím, můžete mi pomoci?*

Index

See also separate indexes for Eating (p125), Sleeping (p125), Shopping (p126) and Sights with map references (p127).

EATING

SLEEPING

SHOPPING

Sights Index

FEATURES

	Eating
	Entertainment, Drinking, Café
	Highlights
	Shopping
	Sights/Activities
	Sleeping

ROUTES

	Tollway
	Freeway
	Primary Road
	Secondary Road
	Tertiary Road
	Lane
	Under Construction
	One-Way Street
	Unsealed Road
	Mall/Steps
	Tunnel
	Walking Path
	Walking Trail
	Track
	Walking Tour

BOUNDARIES

	State, Provincial
	Regional, Suburb
	Ancient Wall

TRANSPORT

	Airport, Airfield
	Bus Route
	Cable-Car, Funicular
	Cycling, Bicycle Path
	Ferry
	General Transport
	Metro
	Monorail
	Rail
	Taxi Rank
	Trail Head
	Tram

AREAS

	Beach, Desert
	Building
	Land
	Mall
	Other Area
	Park/Cemetary
	Sports
	Urban

HYDROGRAPHY

	River, Creek
	Intermittent River
	Canal
	Swamp
	Water

SYMBOLS

	Bank, ATM
	Buddhist
	Castle, Fortress
	Christian
	Diving, Snorkeling
	Embassy, Consulate
	Hospital, Clinic
	Information
	Internet Access
	Islamic
	Jewish
	Lighthouse
	Lookout
	Monument
	Mountain, Volcano
	National Park
	Parking Area
	Petrol Station
	Picnic Area
	Point of Interest
	Police Station
	Post Office
	Ruin
	Telephone
	Toilets
	Zoo, Bird Sanctuary
	Waterfall